LUCIFER

OR
THE TRUE STORY OF THE FAMOUS DIABOLIC POSSESSION IN ALSACE

Compiled from original documents by
ABBÉ PAUL SUTTER
of the diocese of Strasbourg
Translated into English by the
REV. THEOPHILUS BORER

Original Copyright in all British Dominions except Canada
London :
Bouch's Printing Works, Ltd , 98-100, Markhouse Rd. Wahhamstow, E. 17
MCMXXll

Reprint by
Sensus Traditionis Press
2014

Table of Contents

PREFACE   5

INTRODUCTION   3

CHAPTER I
    THIEBAUT AND JOSEPH BURNER   7

CHAPTER II
    THE DEVIL   10

CHAPTER III
    SATAN AND HOLY OBJECTS   12

CHAPTER IV
    SATAN AND THE MOTHER OF CHRIST   17

CHAPTER V
    LOSS OF HEAVEN: PAIN OF HELL   20

CHAPTER VI
    SATAN AND ROWDY AMUSEMENTS, BALLS, DANCES   23

CHAPTER VII
    THE DEVIL AS PROPHET   26

CHAPTER VIII
    NEW PLOTS   34

CHAPTER IX
    THE AGONIES OF THE VICTIMS   37

CHAPTER X
    SATAN'S CONFESSIONS   44

CHAPTER XI
    THE EPISCOPAL COMMISSION   47

CHAPTER XII
>A SCENE AT ST. CHARLES' 50

CHAPTER XIII
>THIEBAUT'S DELIVERANCE 53

CHAPTER XIV
>JOSEPH ALSO IS DELIVERED 60

CHAPTER XV
>VICTORY OF CHRIST'S MOTHER 64

CHAPTER XVI
>WORLDLY WISDOM AND PROFESSORIAL MISCONCEPTIONS 68

APPENDIX
>REPORT OF EPISCOPAL COMMISSION 76

PREFACE

There are many, able men and women, who refuse to believe in the existence of the Devil. They think it a fable, and for those who believe in it they have only ridicule or pity. Yet these very people will readily accept what reason admits as possible and what history attests as true.

This is not the place to give proofs for the existence of the Devil or of spirits good or evil: suffice it to say that reason admits that such beings are possible; faith teaches that they really exist and the history of the human race confirms the teachings of faith.

Even the scope of modern spiritism, apart from its many deceptions, seems to be to show that there is a spirit world.

Wicked spirits can exist just as wicked men can exist, and if they exist they can do us harm if God permits them.

The little book "Lucifer," translated from Abbe Suttor's original Alsatian documents by Father Borer is an authentic record of diabolical possession, of injury done to two innocent children by the Devil.

Should this little book come into the hands of the unbeliever his first impulse will be, perhaps to smile superciliously, and even ridicule those who believe in it, or pity them as weak-minded and the slaves of prejudice.

Let him read this book and he will find that at least it furnishes evidence that any court of Law would admit as proof that something very unnatural happened in the case of these two children.

Unless the existence of the Devil and his power to injure people be admitted, how can what happened to those two Illfurt children be explained? Since the Great War Spiritism has become for many a sort of popular creed: apart from its many deceptions it cannot be denied that it tends to, and often establishes, contact with evil spirits, having sad consequences for many of those who engage in it. It enfeebles the intellect and will, and for some the result is insanity, for others, suicide.

All thoughtful men and women should unite in opposing a practice that has brought such sad consequences to many of its innocent dupes. If the incidents related in the book "Lucifer" will help as a warning to its readers, and their friends, against having any dealings with Spiritism, it will do a useful work, and Father Borer will have conferred a benefit on its English readers by his translation of it.

ST. GEORGE'S, WILLIAM O'GRADY,
WALTHAMSTOW, Vicar-General.
LONDON, E.17.

LUCIFER

INTRODUCTION

On the subject or the existence of evil spiritual beings or devils, the teaching of the Catholic Church is clear and emphatic. The Church teaches that there are bodiless spiritual beings, having intellect and therefore personality, and created by God in a state of sanctifying grace. They were destined by Him to great glory in Heaven. The Almighty, however, gives no one a crown without its having been previously merited by effort. "For he also, that striveth for the mastery, is not crowned except he strive lawfully." (II Timothy 2:5). He subjected all angels to a trial in order to make them deserve as a reward the everlasting happiness. A great number, however, failed in this test of fidelity. They desired, rather, to rival God Himself, and their pride caused them to lose the sanctifying grace of the Holy Spirit. Their sin was a voluntary rebellion against the Almighty: an actual breaking away of them, as created beings, from God their Creator. It was, moreover, a sin committed by beings of intellects immensely greater than those of any *human* beings: for the mental energy and will-power of those pure spiritual creatures (angels) not only enabled them to adhere irrevocably to their purposes, but left them devoid of any excuse of ignorance or weakness. Their sin, then, was of unmixed malice and without possibility of repentance. They immediately thereupon became rejected by God. Their spiritual life faded away in the darkening of their intellects and the hardening of their wills. They lost eternal happiness and their punishment was hell. "For God spared not the angels that sinned : but delivered them, drawn clown by infernal ropes to the lower hell, unto torments, to be reserved unto judgment" (II Peter 2:4).

These malignant spirits are our enemies. They are jealous of us human creatures who, according to St. Thomas, are destined one day to fill their place in Heaven. Unable to prevail against the power of God, they seek to draw men into temptation and sin, with the purpose of separating them from their Maker both in time and in eternity. They began their nefarious work with our first parents, by inciting them to disobey God. This first sin brought Adam and Eve, and all their descendants (with the sole exception of Christ's Mother) into the power and bondage of Satan until Christ the Saviour appeared in this world to destroy, by His Atonement on the Cross, the work of the hellish foe, to break his power and to restore spiritual freedom to fallen mankind. Thereafter, it became possible for man to overcome, with the help of Divine grace, all temptations of the seducer and to obtain eternal happiness in Heaven.

Belief in evil spirits is as old and widespread as humanity itself. Even heathens believed in their existence. The misguided pagan imagination, it is true, disfigured the primal truth, and their fears led them to render Divine honours to the evil geniuses. The Old Testament, again, often mentions the spirits of hell, with their baleful influence in this world and warns men against their malice. Foremost in our mind is the story of patient Job, with the dreadful calamities which Satan was allowed to bring upon the head of that great sufferer.

When Christ appeared on earth, the belief in the devil's existence and harmful influence was general amongst the Jews. Our Lord and His Apostles confirmed that belief by word and by deed. They taught the means of resisting bad spirits and also they themselves expelled those beings from the bodies of people suffering from diabolical possession. The Catholic Church, the pillar and ground of truth (I Timothy 3:15), acts in the same way. She teaches the fact of the existence of fallen angels. She protects the faithful with appropriate spiritual weapons: the sign of the Cross, holy water, etc. She has her own formula of exorcism against diabolic possession. She invests her priests with the power of destroying the might of Satan and of expelling him from possessed bodies.

In His inscrutable designs God allows evil spirits to hurt and frustrate human activities with persistent interference. At times they will injure men in their worldly goods, as witness the cases of holy Iob, St. Anthony the hermit, St. Teresa, the Job, d'Ars, Maria of Mori, Crescentia of Kaufbeuren, etc. This is what is called, in theological language, *obsessio*. It even happens, at times, that Satan is allowed to penetrate into a human body, to unite himself with it and to exercise a real control over its senses, limbs, and organs. This mysterious indwelling enables him to use for his own purposes the senses of his victim, to confuse the spiritual actions of the soul and to produce in this way most strange and wonderful effects (*possessio*).

The marks of true "possession" are as follows:

(1) Knowledge of foreign languages never studied before;
(2) Scientific insight : striking ability, in solving scientific problems, by persons without education;
(3) Knowledge of distant, secret things; penetration into the thoughts of others;
(4) Exhibition of strength far above what is human or natural ;
(5) The "binding" (suspension of the power) of bodily organs, resulting in blindness, deafness, muteness.

Both Bible and Church History relate the frequency of *possessio* in times past. Often Christ freed men from evil spirits. He drove out many devils and forbade them to speak : (Mark 1:34), and the devils left many saying, "Thou art the Son of God": (Luke 4:41). Well known is the case of the two possessed men of Gerasa (Luke 8:31), and that of the possessed boy at the foot of Mount Thabor (Matthew 9:33). The power of exorcism was left by Christ to the Apostles

(Matthew 10:1); and the Church, confirming the teaching of the Apostolic Fathers and of the Doctors in all times, proves her power over possessed men by the fact of exorcism or adjuration; i.e., a solemn command to Satan, in the name of Christ and His holy mother Mary, to quit the bodies of possessed persons or to abstain from acts of enmity against men. The Church has a special consecrated clerical order — *ordo exorcistatus* — whose task it is to expel the devil from unfortunate victims.

Subsequent to the death of Christ on the cross, possession is of rare occurrence in Christian countries. Among the heathens, however, it is even nowadays fairly frequent according to the experience of our missionaries. It does happen, however — though rarely — that the Almighty allows the foe to dwell in a human body and to subject it to all kinds of disorders. Many people are still alive who have witnessed the case of the two boys of Illfurt, in Alsace; and who can establish the actuality of the events affecting those children. Such awful things can never be forgotten.

We have authentic documents, written by eye and ear witnesses who, as experts, have thoroughly investigated the case. They help us to throw the light of fact on the most tragic yet most interesting story of the suffering of these two little Illfurt citizens. The documents are found partly in the archives of the parish, partly in the papers of the ex-*Maire* and deputy, Ignace Spies, of Selestat, and in the writings of Professor Lachemann, both these gentlemen having investigated the case most thoroughly and most conscientiously. The Rev. rector Hausser, who is still alive and who was in those days chaplain of St. Charles' and Monsieur Andre, of Ribeauville, who had charge of the elder boy in the final weeks of his affliction, have also left documentary records of their impressions, which have helped us in our task. A series of articles in the *Revue Catholique* of Alsace, of the year 1870 and a brief history of the case by l'Abbé Brey, the parish priest of Illfurt, have also been consulted.

(*Of course, there is only question, in any, case, of events in the historic sphere, claiming only a human, and not a dogmatic assent).

CHAPTER I
THIEBAUT AND JOSEPH BURNER

In the village of Illfurt, five miles south of Mulhouse, in Alsace, dwelt a poor but respectable family named Burner. Joseph Burner the father, was a traveling merchant who sold matches and tinder. The mother, Mary Ann Poltzer, looked carefully after her five little children. Their eldest son, Thiebaut, was born on August 21, 1855, and the second, Joseph, on April 29, 1857. When eight years old they went to the elementary school. They were quiet boys, somewhat delicate, and of average intelligence. In autumn, 1864, they were both visited by a mysterious malady. Dr. Levy of Alt-Kirch, who was first called upon to diagnose the case, as well as other doctors who were consulted afterwards, were unable to explain the sickness. The remedies prescribed by them had no effect. Thiebaut became thin as a wandering shadow.

From September 25, 1865, the boys displayed most abnormal phenomena. Whilst lying on their backs, they span round in circles like tops, with great rapidity. Then they began to belabour their bedstead and other furniture with astonishing strength and persistence. This they called "thrashing." Never were they tired with their heavy exertions, however long the "thrashing" lasted. They had fits of convulsions and at times such prostrations as to lie down for hours, like corpses, motionless.

It often happened that, when sitting on their wooden chairs, the boys, and also the chairs, were lifted up into the air, and then the boys were thrown into one corner while the chairs were flung into another. At other times they felt all over their bodies a painful pricking and stinging and then they pulled out from beneath their clothes such a great quantity of feathers and seaweed as to cover therewith the whole floor. Frequent change of clothing did nothing in the matter. Always there appeared feathers and seaweed, and these feathers, which covered their bodies so mysteriously, gave out a frightful stench which made it necessary to destroy them. Strange to say, when they were burnt, they left no ashes behind.

Their dreadful convulsions and other sufferings of every kind forced the poor victims to remain in bed with swollen bodies. If perchance an object blessed by the Church — such as a crucifix, sacred medal, or rosary — was shown to them, they flew into a frenzy of rage. They prayed no more. The names of Jesus, Mary, Holy Spirit, pronounced by those who approached them, made them quake and tremble. Spectres, seen by them only, filled them with terror.

Fear came likewise over the poor parents who were obliged helplessly to witness these horrible scenes. Neighbours marveled. Visitors from near and far became more numerous. Everybody wanted to see the poor children. What had happened to them?

There lived at Illfurt an old woman of bad repute who had been expelled from her own native village on account of her profligacy. It is related that from her the two boys had received apples which they had eaten. This is said to have been the origin of their strange illness; even according, as afterwards transpired, to the testimony of the evil spiritual beings thus possessing the bodies of the boys. However this may be, assured facts were soon to prove what kind of power was the origin of the phenomena: for the tree is known by its fruits.

Often the children lay for hours in motionless apathy. Then suddenly their whole being changed. They became nervous and excited and gesticulated and shouted incessantly. Their voices were, however, not those of children, but the strong, rough, hoarse ones of men. Their mouths were then mostly closed and it was evident that they had nothing to do with such language and screams, and that invisible beings were speaking through their mouths. For hours they would scream without ceasing, using, such meaningless phrases as, "Paste threads! Paste knots! Watercress!" The horrible scenes almost forced the onlookers to take to their heels and the poor parents knew not whence to seek help. Most striking was the fear of the children for articles blessed by the Church. Equally great was their antagonism to church, prayer, and religion. Dreadful were their blasphemies, as in their filthy language, they used a vocabulary unknown to them in their normal state. They likewise spoke, and answered fluently, in different languages — French, Latin, English. Even the most varied dialects of French and Spanish were known to them. No wonder that everyone wanted to see the unfortunate children, and that Church and State took an interest in them and investigated their case most thoroughly.

Foremost among the sympathizers, with the unhappy Burner family and its two pitiful children, was the parish priest of the village, the Abbé Brey, a noble and God-fearing priest. His mind was quickly made up as to the diabolic origin of the phenomena. It was a real case of possession. He could not otherwise explain rationally what was taking place. The ecclesiastical authority was communicated with, and a committee of enquiry, consisting of three theologians, was appointed for the purpose of officially investigating the case and of taking in hand, later on, the task of exorcism. The Abbé Brey was strongly supported by the *Maire* and the best families of the village. Sceptics were, of course, still to be found, but their number was small. For them the hellish spirits showed sympathy, whereas they hated those who saw through their nature. A special object of their aversion were the parish priest and the *Maire*. They also showed great hatred for Monsieur Ignace Spies, the *Maire* of Selestat, his friend M. Martinot, directeur de regie of the same town, and for Professor Lachemann, a *frère de Marie* of St. Hippolyte. These three gentlemen had come from a distance to study the case in its minutest details.

CHAPTER II
THE DEVIL

Each boy was infested by at least two bad spirits. These concealed their names as long as they could, but Father Souquat forced them in Christ's name to reveal their identity. *Oribas* and *Ypes* were raging in the elder boy, Thiebaut. Ypes called himself a hellish chieftain ruling over seventy-one legions. One of the spirits who haunted the younger boy, Joseph, named himself *Solalethiel*; the name of Joseph's other tormentor, unfortunately, cannot be remembered. This Solalethiel surpassed in cunning and cruelty the devils of Thiebaut. Ypes was struck with deafness for so long as he dominated his hapless victim. The latter had completely lost the sense of hearing, so as not to be in the least affected even by pistols being fired in the closest proximity to his ears. He recovered this sense only when delivered from his foe.

The evil spirits had their own superiors and masters, before whom they trembled. They received occasional calls from them which were not welcome.

"Now comes the master!" was once the terrified cry of one of the boys.

"What master?" he was asked.

"Our chief!"

"Is he stronger than you?"

"Oh, yes!"

"What is his appearance?"

"He has two feet, a body covered with feathers, a long neck, and a beak like a duck's. His hands resemble the claws of a cat!"

"Hold him when he comes!" cried an onlooker. On this, the boy shouted, "Here he is! Here he is!" With the "master" came other spirits, his lieutenants. "There are many of us!" then exclaimed the possessed boy.

At times this great chief appeared in the form of a wild man, of a dog, or also of a serpent.

CHAPTER III
SATAN AND HOLY OBJECTS

The diabolic nature of the malady, which was afflicting the boys, revealed itself especially when the latter were brought into proximity to holy water, or medals or rosaries which had been blessed according to the ritual. Then the indwelling spirits caused the boys to rage, to froth at the mouth and to struggle with the utmost energy to avoid coming in contact with such article. Food, mingled with some drops of holy water, they would never touch, although the fact of mixing was unknown to them. "Away with this filthy stuff!" they would cry; "it is poisoned!" To endeavours at forcible feeding they would oppose frantic resistance, aiming blows right and left and clenching their teeth immovably. Food, unmixed with any holy water, however, they would accept and devour eagerly. A strange fact, however, was that it was necessary to induce them to eat their food by putting it into their mouths with three fingers "because," the evil spirit had once declared, "what *the little dog* [meaning the boy!] eats with his left hand, or with only two fingers of his right, belongs to me, and not to him!"

A neighbour, Madame Brobeck, had secretly put some holy

water into their medicine. "We would rather take all the phials of the druggist than the slightest taste of this filth!" cried the possessed boy. On another occasion they were presented with figs which had been previously blessed according to ecclesiastical form. "Away with the *ratheads*! The priest has made grimaces over them!" shouted one of the boys.

On one occasion Monsieur Spies held before the eyes of one of the boys a small relic of St. Gerard Majella, and said, "Look! This Saint has put to flight many of thy tribe!" Immediately, the boy grimaced, puffed his cheeks and held his lips tightly closed. Just then the relic was pressed on to his lips. The boy resisted with all his strength, whirled round and behaved like a man in despair. At last he cried out, "Clear out, you Italian!" Gerard Majella was, indeed, a young Italian Redemptorist brother, who had died in the odour of sanctity. The possessed boy had no natural means of knowing this.

What the Satanic spirit dreaded most was the blessed medal of St. Benedict. For that reason, almost every parishioner of Illfurt endeavoured to obtain one and carry it on his person.

Once, Monsieur Tresch was reading from a prayer book in the presence of the boys. He was interrupted by them. "It is not necessary," they exclaimed, "for you to come here to speak of the *Païas* on the Cross and of the *Great Lady*!" In these terms they referred to our blessed Lord and His holy mother!

They displayed a most awful dread of the Blessed Virgin Mary. One day, Monsieur Tresch put a medal of Our Lady of Perpetual Succour into the ear of the deaf boy and ordered the Satanic spirit to depart. The child exclaimed : "I cannot! Behold, yonder, sulphur, resin, and pitch !"

When the nursing sister brought him something to eat and to drink, after having secretly mingled with it some holy water, the boy refused the food: or, as a rule, he would fling the dish or the glass against the wall but without breaking them. On such an occasion, a young man of the village came into the room and approached Thiebaut's bed. The possessed boy looked at him and said, "Yes, eating and drinking and leading a bad life: this is thy way to Heaven!" The terrified youth scampered away!

Before Monsieur Tresch left the boy, he sprinkled the bed with holy water, pronouncing the formula prescribed in the ritual: "*Sit nomen Domini benedictum*"! ("Blessed be the name of the Lord"). "*Non sit!*" groaned the Satanic spirit in the possessed boy!

One day, a priest put a blessed medal on the ear of one of the boys whilst he was asleep. Suddenly, the ear began to shake, until the medal had fallen away. The same thing happened when the medal was placed on the head.

When the boy succeeded in hiding away any blessed article, he would grin and say, "Look now for thy filthy thing! It is stinking!"

Towards priests the Satanic spirit was always full of hatred, pouring upon them the grossest insults and most opprobrious epithets, such as might be learnt from the edifying talk of the most extreme and fanatical partizans of the enemies of religion: "*Black-cowls! Skunks! Sorcerers!*" — these were amongst the less violent of the names!

He honoured with especial derision Monsieur le Superieur Stumpf. "I am going now to harass *Stumpflé*, the stinkpot!" he cried on one occasion, adding after a while, "I have played a fine trick on him ! If only I had been able to *do him in!*" When asked about the incident, M. le Superieur stated that, at that very moment, he was lifted into the air by an invisible force, that all his pictures were flung from the wall, that his furniture was moved and thrown about, and that uncanny phenomena appeared in his room until he sprinkled everything with holy water and commanded the hellish spirits in God's name to leave him in peace. This statement was confirmed by the Satanic spirit itself. "*Stumpflé!*" said he: "Stumpflé, the miserable, has barred me from the entrance by smearing his room all over with filth!"

The Satanic entity had much greater sympathy for members of Jewish and Freemasonic sects. "They are good people!" he said, sometimes; "All ought to be what they are! They go in for true liberty! They save our 'master' a lot of trouble and gain many people for him! The *dung-beetles* [this epithet referred to the Catholics] however, and the *black-cowls* [clergy !] do him much damage and snatch many souls from him!"

The Satanic spirit displayed a passionate hatred of the clerical *soutane* and of the religious habit. He flew from the very touch of either, whereas he had no objection to being covered, by a layman, with his overcoat or other garment.

Once the spirit, speaking through his unhappy boy victim, said to Monsieur Tresch : "When you go to the *pigsty* [church !] and lift up your hands and *blubber* [pray !], your destiny is above [pointing towards the sky], whereas those, who do not follow you, come to us."

A lady visitor from Bettendorf put, one day whilst the boy's hands were tightly clasped, a blessed rosary on his breast. He shouted furiously. "If I can get hold of those *balls* [beads !] I'll tear to pieces the *cat-tail* [chain is connecting the rosary-beads!], but I must not touch the image of the *Great Lady* [the Blessed Virgin] which is suspended from it!"

"What," he was asked, "is engraved on the medal."

"A boy and a girl, protected by the Great Lady," he replied. On enquiry, the medal in question was found to be one of La Salette, representing the appearance of the Blessed Virgin to the two children of La Salette.

A lay person, who witnessed this scene, repeated devoutly the liturgical prayer, "From the snares of the devil deliver us, O Jesus !" Upon hearing this sound of supplication, the possessed boy flew into an appalling rage. "Be silent!" he cried, "Thou art lying! Shut up!"

On the occasion of a Corpus Christi procession, the behaviour of the diabolic spirit was simply unutterable. One of the afflicted boys was taken into a house in front of which the Blessed Sacrament altar was set up. The diabolic entity caused him to shout, bluster, and rave in such a way that the appalling scene became unendurable. He only calmed himself when the procession was over.

Similar incidents took place, although in a lesser degree, whenever the poor children were brought into contact with a crucifix, a rosary, or any other blessed object. It was always the same dread, the same horror, the same blasphemies, the same fury. It all proves the astonishing power and effects of the sacramentals, which, in the hands of faithful Christians, are an excellent weapon against the attacks and temptations of the hellish foe.

CHAPTER IV
SATAN AND THE MOTHER OF CHRIST

Whilst the fallen angel insulted and be-mocked everything holy, not even excepting God Himself, he never had the courage of assailing Mary, the mother of our Lord Jesus Christ. Asked for the reason of such surprising behaviour, he always answered, "I cannot do it. The *Païas on the tree* [the diabolic spirit's extraordinary name for Christ!] has forbidden it." He always referred to the Blessed Virgin as "the Great Lady."

During a momentary calm, the boy Thiebaut was given a framed picture of our Lady, and he played harmlessly with it. Suddenly there came the crisis. With all his strength he flung the picture to the floor, where it was smashed to pieces. Professor Lachemann, a *frère de Marie*, who happened to be there, put to him the following question in Latin, whilst others forced the boy to be quiet, "*Quid sentis de Immaculata Conceptione Beatae Mariae Virginis quae contrivit caput tuum?*"—("What thinkest thou concerning the Immaculate Conception of the Blessed Virgin Mary, who has crushed thy head?"). In a paroxysm of rage, the diabolic being caused the possessed boy groaningly to reply, "Get away! Go away, with your Great Lady! I want to know nothing about her!".

Then he began to curse and blaspheme in so monstrous a way, that the nursing sister, who was also present, was inexpressibly terrified. She made the sign of the cross with holy water three times: upon the boy's forehead, mouth, and breast, mentioning at the same time the name of the Blessed Trinity. This was sufficient to bring back the patient to a quiet composure.

Let it be remarked here that, at the instance of the parish priest, Abbé Brey, two religious sisters from Niederbronn, Sister Severa and Sister Methula, watched and nursed both children without respite. Very difficult was their task! Horrible was their experience! To what innumerable frightful things they had to listen!

In his conversations with Monsieur Tresch, the possessed boy repeatedly mentioned the "Great Lady" whom he [M. Tresch] "keeps at home in a shrine." "But you have never seen her!" answered the *Maire*. "Yet I know," exclaimed the boy, "that you give everything to the Great Lady and to her *dog* [thus blasphemously alluding to Christ!]. You carry her always in your pocket !"

"But why do you call them such awful names ?" asked the good Christian.

"I cannot," replied the possessed boy, "do otherwise."

One day, Messieurs Spies and Martinot, accompanied by Monsieur Tresch, entered the house of the possessed children. The latter had seen them coming down the road and the sight had very much irritated them. They were scarcely in the room when little Joseph opened the conversation with Mons. Tresch. "You have sent a letter to *Spitz* [a nickname for Mons. Spies—another such name was *Canisi*] and this man here [Martinot], has come with you."

"I have not written," assured the *maire*.

"You have," persisted the boy, "and the other one accompanied him." This was, indeed, a fact. Then both boys began to tremble and Thiebaut shouted in French, "*Liberté, egalité, fraternité République française!* (The coming *République* seemed more agreeable to the possessing entity than did the then existing Empire).

Monsieur Spies took the little Joseph on his knees and questioned him on various subjects. Sometimes the answers were correct. Often also, however, he would say, "You have no right to know that." Mention was likewise made of things concerning which the dark prince disliked to speak. "What," the evil spirit was asked, "have you done with Voltaire, since he came down to you?"

"Ah!" was the reply. "We received him with great pomp. We went in *cropsession* [procession] to meet him; but we held him fast! When he approached the gate of hell, he got frightened and looked as though he wanted to retrace his steps; but he could not escape us, and we forced him to enter *the Fireholer*."

Whilst still holding the children on his knees, Mons. Spies placed, on the back of the head of one of them, a piece of silk, which the child could neither see nor even feel. On a sudden, the boy exclaimed, "Put this *rag* away! It burns me!"—and he tried to rid himself of his visitor. "But it is not a rag," answered Mons. Spies; "I will take it from you, if you will tell me what is on it."

"Take it from me ! It burns me," replied the possessed boy.

"I shall not remove it," responded Mons. Spies, "so long as you do not tell me what is on it, no matter how much you gesticulate!"

"The *Great Lady* is on it!" exclaimed the boy, in tones of terror. And, indeed, it really was a picture of our Lady, painted on silk!

Again, the boy cried in beseeching accents, "Throw away what you carry in your pocket! It burns me!" He meant the little crucifix which the deputy had with him, and of the presence of which the boy had no natural means of knowing. "There are *relics* in it!" he said; and it was a fact!

Even the medals Mons. Spies carried round his neck annoyed him and, he said, "burned" him!

CHAPTER V
LOSS OF HEAVEN: PAIN OF HELL

The thoughts of having lost Heaven forever made Satan inexpressibly unhappy. On several occasions, through the mouths of the two afflicted boys, the evil spirit sighed: "How beautiful it is, there above!   How beautiful! Oh, if only it were granted to me to see again that glory, how happy I should be!"

Another time he said: "What a beauty there is in Heaven! Could I only be allowed to see it once! But no! Never shall I see it again!"

"Why do you manifest such an ardent longing?" asked Monsieur Tresch.

"I am," he declared enigmatically, "forced to do so, by the Three who are stronger than me."   After Thiebaut had been conveyed to St. Charles's Institute at Schiltigheim, he remained quiet and silent for the first three days. In the evening of the fourth day, the devil again showed itself in him. "I am here!" He exclaimed suddenly, "and I am in a rage!" The nursing sisters then asked him who he was. "I am," he replied, "a prince of darkness!"

"Where," the Sister continued, "is thy home?"

"In hell!"

"Would you like to go to heaven?"

"Oh, yes!" cried the possessing demon. "But there is no hope of admission!"

"Who has expelled you," the Sister asked, "from Heaven?"

"Michael!" cried the infuriated fiend. "Michael, the *stinker*! With his sword!"

"What would you be prepared to do to go to Heaven?"

"I'd crawl," replied the spirit, "for a thousand years on points of needles, and slide on keenly sharpened knives!" He added that he was a hellish chieftain commanding a legion of devils in the air, the immense number of which would obscure the light of the sun and they had bodies like men!

"The teaching of the Catholic Church as to hell," the spirit declared, "is true; but hellfire," he added, "is far above what you can conceive it to be! It is beyond your power of comprehension. Its heat is greater and more active! It causes indescribable agony!"

Then the evil demon almost invariably expressed the wish that he could be annihilated by Almighty God.

Once he was asked for information as to the language spoken in hell. Then, with great bombast and uncanny rapidity, the boy, under the influence of the possessing spirit, came out with a jargon which sounded like a mixture of Italian and Latin, with the often-recurring and clearly distinguishable word, "*Victoria!*"

"That," he continued, speaking now in German, "is the language spoken there."

"Where, there?" interrupted Monsieur Tresch. "In hell ?"

"Yes. In hell!"

In the evening of March 28 the possessed boy described the Passion of Christ. Mentioning the Agony in the Garden, he suddenly exclaimed, "Indeed Thou art hot; frightfully hot! Thou art bathed in sweat for the sins of men!" The evil spirit likewise acknowledged his presence at the crucifixion of Christ, where he incited the Jews to torture our Lord, and counted all the blows that fell upon Him. A visitor then asked, "What does hell look like?"

"Not nice !" he answered. On further queries being put, he became impatient, and said, "This is no business of yours. Try to get there and you'll know by personal experience!"

Now and then, the Satanic spirit endeavoured to make some little "propaganda" for himself! To a visitor he offered a daily bribe of 100 francs to enter his service! Even poor Burner, the head of the terrorised family, was asked to serve him, for the sum of 1000 francs! To Monsieur Tresch he said, one day, "I possess many sackfuls of gold and silver and I will help you to find them!"

"All right," replied Monsieur Tresch ; "I am pleased to hear it! I shall give the treasure partly to the Church and partly to the poor!"

"No ! No !" the fiendish being caused the boy to shout. "That is not what I mean!"

Does not all this sound almost like the voice of Christ's tempter in the desert (Matthew 4:9) : "All these will I give Thee, if falling down Thou wilt adore me"? This proud and most unhappy spirit of darkness has no greater longing than to see all men pressed into his service!

CHAPTER VI
SATAN AND ROWDY AMUSEMENTS, BALLS, DANCES

The possessed boys had, frequently, intervals (and even whole days) of relative tranquillity. The evil spirits were then absent from them and the children would eat, drink, talk and play just like their comrades. They remembered nothing of the dreadful happenings during the possession. As a rule, His Satanic Majesty gave himself leave of absence on Sunday afternoons. When, at the beginning of a subsequent crisis, he was asked where he had been, he would reply : "In such and such a neighbouring village, at the annual fair! Fine doings there!"

"I have," he would continue, "played them grand tricks, and reaped an abundant harvest! This is my greatest pleasure, and I take delight in stirring up passions and in encouraging wicked amusements of young people."

At St. Charles's Institute he said once, "I want a drink." Monsieur Andre thereupon said, "Thou canst not drink! Thou art a spirit! What beverage canst thou wish for! Clear out of here and go back to hell!" The devilish being replied, "I sit down with drinkers and incite them to excessive indulgence until they get drunk. In this state of stupidity they spill some liquor on the table or floor, and that waste is mine!" (The demon declared, furthermore, his liking for balls and dances, since, at such functions, he had ample opportunities of tempting young people there into snares and fooleries.

After this conversation with Monsieur Andre, the spirit left the body of the possessed boy. Ten minutes later, he returned and said, with malignant laughter, "I have just come from the Beerhouse."

Speaking under the influence of the possessing demon, the boy spoke of a certain public house and its proprietor, as well as of other inns and innkeepers at Schiltigheim, although he had never been in that village before. Then he said, "I am doing well, and can rejoice! My master will be pleased with me. It happens only too often, alas, that in such houses the language is ambiguous and obscene. Then the demoniac spirit was in his element: Nothing gave him greater joy!" One day, some half-drunken lads were disputing angrily whilst passing the Institute.

"Wait!" the evil spirit suddenly cried. "I am going to get up a good fight!" Five minutes later, furious blows were raining on the youths and the row was repeated three times. Meanwhile, the possessed boy was laughing heartily.

One day, the spirit suddenly interrupted the babble of the afflicted boy, and shouted, "Silence! We have got him!"

"Whom have you caught ?" he was asked. The demon replied: "The young man who is dancing at the public house in Selestat [he named the precise locality]. Now we have him!" he shouted; "Now he is with us!"

Immediate enquiries proved that, at the same hour and place that had been named by the demon, a young man, whilst dancing, had been seized with an apoplectic fit and fallen dead on the floor!

When at Illfurt, the spirit one day said, "This blockhead [*dieser Bock*] of N. and his wife have gone to the pigsty [*Schweinestall*] for a feed [*um zu fressen*]! [The demon meant, they had gone to church to Communion]. They were," he continued, "hungry ! Scarcely had they come home than they began to quarrel and curse in a mad frenzy, the most appalling blasphemies coming from them like snowflakes [wie Schneeflocken]. It was a treat to me! I laughed in perfect delight! In the evening they could have again gone back to the *Schweinestall*, for their state was worse than in the morning! I have placed all their curses in a small box, where I keep them!" Blasphemies, cursing, quarrelling, objectionable feasts, dances, balls : all these the Satanic spirit praised beyond measure.

CHAPTER VII
THE DEVIL AS PROPHET

From what has been related in this narrative, it is evident that the devilish beings know what happens at great distances and even in far away countries. They have, also, expert knowledge of world history. The spirit, which possessed one of the boys, often revealed things of a far-removed past, which could not have been known by any natural means. More than that, he predicted coming events days and weeks beforehand. These events subsequently occurred as foretold, to the amazement of everyone! (Fallen angels do not lose all their knowledge; as a matter of fact, we poor mortals cannot even imagine the extent of their craftiness and intellectual accumen!).

Visitors were often told, in the minutest detail, the evils — even the most secret sins — they had committed! They could not stand it and they disappeared with the greatest possible haste!

At times, he even attempted to lecture people for their moral defects! To a neighbour he said, "You toper! Were you not present when the priest was preaching against drunkenness? Yet you have gone to N... to get a tippler's nose. You are the cause of your daughter's illness and of your cattle's disease!" On Palm Sunday he gave a good scolding to a native of Illfurt : "You swiller! Did you not hear the priest in the *Schweinestall* [thus repeating his epithet for "church"!] say nobody must go to the public house this week? Your obedience is edifying indeed! Have you not been with the baker of Flacksianden in the tavern at X...? Have you not imbibed a copious quantity of beer?"

Other people had to expiate even more severely the cravings of curiosity. Pale, as though struck, by lightning, they fled away terrified: for the demon had revealed to them mysteries of an evil nature and had charged them with serious offences, committed in former days, and which they had imagined to be quite unknown to anyone but themselves!

The *Maire* of a village in the neighbourhood of Strasbourg said once to his Councillors, after a municipal meeting, "Gentlemen, who goes with me next Sunday to Schiltighein? We will go to see the possessed boy." Several men agreed with the proposal. "But listen, M. le Maire," remarked one of them; "We are told that Satan may there put the flashlight of truth on our own lives!"
"Tomorrow is Saturday," replied the *Maire*. "We'll go to confession; then, at the first Mass on Sunday, we'll go to Holy Communion! We shall then be all right, and the devil can reproach us with nothing!"

This was agreed to and done. On Sunday, they went to Schiltighein and arrived at St. Charles's. They rang the bell. A nursing-sister appeared and enquired their errand. "We should like very much to see the possessed child," answered the *Maire*. "Come with me, gentlemen," she responded. "I'll show you the way." No sooner had the Sister opened the fateful door than the possessed boy cried: " Look here! The *Maire* of X..., with his *Adjoint* and others of the Council, are approaching. You did not trust your good stars, otherwise you would not have gone to church yesterday to scrape the filth from your conscience! But one of you has not done it well! There is a former *beetroot* thief here!"

The man referred to became terrified. His cheeks went red and glowing. He stammered out: " Yes, but I have put on the ground the money to cover the expense of what I took!"

"The owner never had it !" grinned the Satanic spirit.

"Gentlemen, let us go !" said the *Maire*. "He may otherwise reproach me with something unpleasant!"

In a trice the company had disappeared. When, however, the incident was more widely known, the exposed beetroot thief became the laughing stock of all!

Thiebaut predicted several persons' deaths. Two hours before the passing away of a woman, he knelt on his bed and imitated the actions of a bell-ringer at a funeral. On another occasion, he likewise "Tolled" concerning a man who died on the following day, and his effort was so exhausting that he was bathed in sweat.

On Saturday, the eve of the third Sunday of Lent, he foretold that next day several hundred people would arrive (the rumour having spread of the children's deliverance). This happened. That evening, Satan was in an exultant mood, and shouted for joy because so many people had missed their Sunday Mass on account of him!

He mentioned events, which had happened twenty, thirty, even a hundred years before, with such certainty and accuracy as could not have been excelled had he been a personal witness to these happenings. Monsieur Tresch was nominated to the Mayorality of Illfurt in January, 1869. Nobody in the district knew of the appointment. The possessed boy, however, addressed him already as "*Monsieur le Maire*." Indeed, he had previously said to his mother, "I am so furious, that I am almost bursting!"

"And why?" asked the woman.

"Because *the skunk* has been made *Maire*! I, and *our lot*, are frantic with rage!" It was the hour when the nomination papers were forwarded from the prefecture of Colmar!

When Monsieur Tresch entered his room, the boy shouted, "You are a Churchman! You have been at 'Siedlen' [Einsiedeln]."

"You are telling a fib !" retorted Monsieur Tresch. "Tell me where I have been!"

"In Stadt [the town]."

"What Stadt?" asked Monsieur Tresch.

"In Schlett [Selestat]," responded the demon. This was a fact. The demon, speaking through the boy, went on: "You have also seen *the rag-gatherers* [*Lumpensammler*; this abusive term he used as a nickname for the Capuchin fathers], and you have *brought them money that they may make rubbish* [*bast ihnen Geld gebracht, um Lumpen zu machen*; abusive terms in which the demon alluded to offerings for Masses]."

In very deed, Monsieur Tresch shortly before called at the Capuchin monastery of Dornach, near Basel, and had asked the Reverend Guardian to say two Masses for the deliverance of the boys. Not a living soul in Illfurt knew about it, except Monsieur Brobeck, who had accompanied him!

In a particularly grave crisis, the possessing demon revealed that several priests [mentioning their names and parishes] had written about him to the civil and ecclesiastical authorities. "The cleric of X..., and of Z..., have," he said, "communicated with the *High Cleric who wears the hood* [bishop] and the man with the great cap [mitre] has sent word to Mulhouse concerning the *two little dogs* [the possessed boys]." Then, turning towards one of the Sisters who had watched him : "And you bawler," he continued, "you, with your *Geissenbollen and Katzenwadel* [abusive epithets for Rosaries], you shall not sleep three nights longer in the little adjoining room." All persons present were amazed: especially the Sisters, who had not the least idea of their impending removal. That same evening, a letter came from the convent, ordering the nuns to leave the children within two days, and return back to Mulhouse.

One day, little Joseph said to Monsieur Tresch, "I want to recall an incident of your youth. You went to the Forest to hew wood. A snake crawled near."

"What did I do to it?" queried Monsieur Tresch.

"You killed it, under the invocation of *the three names* [the Holy Trinity]," replied the possessing fiend. "And do you know you killed one of my companions? Had you not invoked the three names whilst slaying him, you would have wandered about all night without finding your way out of the wood!" Monsieur Tresch remembered the incident well !

Often did the possessed boy mention events of the beginning of the human race, quite in harmony with the Scripture account. He was present, he said, at the fall of our first parents, and at the destruction of Sodom and Gomorrah. "You would not be obliged to *bawl* [pray] and to *whisper through the grate* [confess] if I had not plucked an apple for Eve." Now and then he went back to past times. "During the Swedish war," he said once, "the *old Schweinestall* (the demon's term for the cemetery church!] was not destroyed, but the priest was killed at the Altar whilst holding aloft the monstrance. Then a soldier tried to behead the statue of the Great Lady. He could not, but fell backward and died. I took him, and many others, with me! The Great Lady allows no stealing from the *Schweinestall*!"

He gave, also, details of awful crimes committed at Illfurt in former times. It was March 12, 1868; Monsieur Tresch was again with the children, and found them fairly quiet. Suddenly, the wicked one manifested his presence. "Here am I !" he shouted, with a strange, hoarse, man's voice.

"Where do you come from?"– asked Monsieur Tresch.

"From Garell."

"Who is he?"

"A bookbinder."

"Where from?"

"From the place of your two visitors."

"What two visitors?" asked Monsieur Tresch.

"The tall one and the old one," replied the demon.

"What are their names ?"

"Canisi ! [Monsieur Spies]," answered the demon.

"Canisi, and, as to the other one, I do not know it. He disgusts me !"

"What," asked Monsieur Tresch, "were you doing at the bookbinder's?"

"I have spent the whole day with him. He has bound a beautiful book, which he looked through with delight. That made me happy and I remained with him all day long."

"Does," asked Monsieur Tresch, "the bookbinder live far away from my tall friend?"

"No. Only the distance of a few houses."

"Do you visit the tall one?"

"No. His door is too low for me to get through."

"What frightens you there?" asked Monsieur Tresch.

"The *Great Lady* who stands outside."

"And my other friend, the 'old one': how do you treat him?"

"I want to know nothing about him! He sickens me!" exclaimed the demon.

"Do you not visit him?"

"No. He carries a round object which prevents me from calling on him!"

"Is it not," asked Monsieur Tresch, "the cross you once saw here?"

"No! It is something which the priest holds aloft, and this would sting me if I went to him!" This was a relic of the Holy Cross, contained in a silver cruciform case.

Monsieur Tresch immediately sent an account of this talk to Monsieur Spies, who went, to the bookbinder — almost his neighbour, in the same street, the Rittergasse and asked him whether, on such and such a day he had not bound a book, and read in it.

Monsieur Garell, whose memory was unreliable, looked through his register and declared that, on that day, he had bound a Bible for the Lutheran pastor of Selastat and that he had read some pissages in it. His visitor, after receiving this information, showed him the letters from Illfurt. "How comes it," exclaimed the astounded bookbinder, that Satan concerns himself with me?"

"Nothing to be astonished at!" replied the visitor. "Faith teaches us that Satan goeth round about like a roaring lion seeking whom he may devour." He then explained to him something of the nature of the evil spirits and their mischievous influence on the destiny of men.

An extraordinary exhibition of occult knowledge occured on July 24,1798. A very zealous priest, a native of Illfurt, Abbé Jean Bochelen, then curate of Niedersept, was condemned to death by the Revolutionary Tribunal of Colmar, for the alleged offence of violating the Emigration Law, but, in reality, out of hatred of the Catholic faith. The holy man was shot dead that same evening, in the sandpit just outside the town. His belongings were kept by his friends like holy relics. His bloodstained shirt remained in the

Bochelen family.

On June 28, 1842, a terrible fire broke out at Illfurt and one of the houses belonging to the Bochelens became a prey to the flames. However, the box containing the letters of the martyred priest and also his breviary, chalice, and other belongings, were saved. The bloody shirt, however, was, in the confusion, carried off by a thief.

All enquiries as to the whereabouts of the relic were fruitless. One day, Professor Lachemann asked the boy Thiebaut, in the presence of Monsieur Tresch: "Say, Thiebaut, do you know Bochelen?"

"Do not mention to me that fighting knight!" answered the possessed. "I want to know nothing about him! Thirty years hence, at his exhumation, his name will be spoken of with reverence by all tongues!"

Three decades later, in 1897, there was published the Abbé Soltner's book "*Jean Bochelen, the Last Alsatian Martyr of the French Revolution,*" by which the memory of this holy priest was rescued from oblivion and his virtues again glorified!

Not long after the publication of that book, a beautiful monument was erected to his memory. It was placed opposite the new presbytery in his native village of Illfurt. A few days after the first mention of the name, Bochelen, to the possessed boy, one of the members of the family to which the martyred priest belonged, asked Thiebaut, "Say! What has become of the shirt of Bochelen?" "Hold thy tongue!" screeched the devil. "A good boy [*good* in Satan's eye!] has stolen it, otherwise it would later on have been made into relic-covers!"

Memorial Column, Illfurt.

L'Abbé Ch. Brey.

CHAPTER VIII
NEW PLOTS

Pitiful beyond expression were the tortures of the poor boys! The hellish master tormented them horribly, especially when his fury was roused by the sight of a blessed medal or other holy object. Then the poor victims tore and smashed to pieces all that came within reach. Any effort at mastering this rage was opposed with utmost strength and it was often enormously difficult to overcome it. Repeatedly Satan declared that he much preferred to dwell in a strong, grownup man, because it would be more difficult to overcome him there, but, when haunting the body of a child, he was allowed to use only such strength as befitted that more feeble body.

Monsieur Tresch, almost a daily visitor, was a subject of the lost angel's great aversion. "I have a bone to pick with you," he one day said. Shortly after, one of Monsieur Tresch's cows broke a leg, "Something already!" said the spirit: "But this is not all!" A few days afterwards, two calves died. "Something else!" grinned the demon: "But I have not finished with him yet !" After a certain time, the *Maire* fell down his staircase and broke his forearm. When this misfortune happened, the fallen angel, with scornful laughter, was already detailing it to the visitors! In the month of May, 1868, Monsieur Tresch had purchased a pig. The next day, this erstwhile healthy animal lost all appetite and began to pine away. The veterinary surgeon not being able to locate any disease, M. le Maire determined to investigate in other ways. He placed in the sty a blessed medal of St. Benedict. Immediately, the animal was well again and took its food as usual. At his next visit to the possessed boy, the enemy gave him a word of explanation. "I am not able to enter thy house any more," he said, "we are obliged to fly away over it. The *filth* [so he described holy objects suspended in houses] prevents our entry."

In several other Illfurt houses the evil being likewise made uncanny noises, especially in the home of Monsieur Kleiber Benjamin. This family had much to endure from him; for example, on one occasion when they called a priest to bless some farm buildings. In the Brobeck and Zurbach families the evil spirit also caused much annoyance. Having had, in an upper room, an infernal witches' vigil, he boasted exultantly: "Did you not hear last night? We made a row to deafen your ears!"

He delighted greatly in causing the poor boys to trace figures of dogs and snakes. "Such we have in hell!" he added: "They are our masters!" One day, Thiebaut was complaining to the nursing sister: "I am covered with lice." She looked and saw that numberless red lice did indeed appear! Immediately she began, with the assistance of three visitors, to belabour his head with brush and comb. The more vermin they destroyed, however, the more appeared! The boy's father became impatient and cried: "Wait, Satan! I will drive your emissaries away!" He fetched holy water, sprinkled the head of the child, and said, "In the name of the Blessed Trinity, I command thee to leave this boy!" Immediately, the creatures disappeared! The same remedy was used on behalf of the other boy, Joseph, who likewise had begun to complain of a similar affliction.

If a visitor came into the room without some sacred emblem on his person, it very commonly happened that his watch stopped, on which occurrence the Satanic spirit jeered. "Why do you not play this trick on *me*?" once asked Monsieur Tresch. "If only I could!"

cried the demon: "I'd do so with joy!"

During summer of 1868, the boys were left quiet for some time. On the return of the crisis, Mr. Tresch asked the diabolic possessor where he had been. "I have been on many errands."

"Have you been in Spain [a revolution was sweeping that country]?"

"Yes!" replied the demon. "There we were most busy! There many have fallen."

"Had you a hand in chasing away the Queen?" asked Monsieur Tresch.

"Oh, surely!"

"And why?"

"In Spain there is a priest almost in every house!"

"Are there really so many priests there?"

"Oh, yes!" cried the demon. "More than here!" Then he added: "If only I could win *thee* over, and the priests here, to my cause, I could stay here; but you are obstinate, and so are *Spitz* [the demon's name for Monsieur Spies] of Selestat and the great, bawler [his epithet for Martinot]!"

"Say," asked Monsieur Tresch, "is it not true that Mary, the Mother of Christ, prays for me and I am protected in my constant opposition to thee?"

"Hold thy tongue! Be silent!" commanded the fiend, in a fury. The demon confessed also that he assisted the great murderer, Troppmann, in his crimes.

CHAPTER IX
THE AGONIES OF THE VICTIMS

The sufferings of the boys could be likened to a continual martyrdom. Even a glance at them inspired terror and pity. During the two first years, in which they were obliged to remain mostly in bed, they often crossed their legs, in most unnatural manner, and entwined them rope-like, so strongly that they could not be pulled one from the other. Then suddenly, with speed of lightning, they bounded back to their freedom.

Often, they stood on head and feet at the same time, with their bodies right upward: a position from which they could not be changed by any outside pressure until it pleased the devilish master to withdraw. When in bed, the boys often traced on the wall horrible caricatures of fiendish faces, to which they spoke and sported. If a rosary were placed on their bed during sleep, they immediately disappeared under the clothes, only reappearing when the beads were removed.

Often, when seated in a chair, the boy was lifted by an invisible power, was then either let fall or else was flung into one corner of the room, while the chair was cast into the other. His mother, seated once with him on a bench, experienced the same fright, but, though thrown against the wall, was uninjured.

Frequently the poor boy's body swelled to bursting point, then he vomited sea froth, feathers, and seaweed. Feathers were likewise seen on his garments, which gave forth a very bad odour. At times, the boys climbed, with feline agility, to the remotest boughs of trees in the garden, without, however, breaking them. In the living room, where there was no oven, the heat occasionally became so unbearable, that people expressed agonized amazement. Thereupon, the evil spirit would say, "I am a good stoker, am I not? Is it not hot near me?"

The mother, who slept in the same room, sometimes was quite unable to endure the heat. She then rose, sprinkled the lads and herself with holy water, and the normal temperature came back! The same happened to the nuns who were watching the patients. What must be the ire of God's anger that torments the lost angels in perdition? The words of the prophet recur to one's mind: "Which of you can dwell with devouring fire, which of you shall dwell with everlasting burnings." (Isaias 33:14).

The good nuns, Sisters Severa and Methula, had a frightful task in watching over and tending the boys. They saw window curtains torn down by invisible hands and closed windows burst open with strange rapidity. They witnessed chairs being overturned: also tables and other furniture being moved, by spirit hands, all over the room. Sometimes, the house shook, as though by an earthquake.

When a priest, or other pious Catholic, made a call, the possessed boys crept in all haste under the table or the bed or leapt from the window. On the other hand, visits from so-called "liberal Christians" gave them great joy. "He is one of ours!" they would shout: "What a boon if all were like them!"

After Thiebaut's arrival at St. Charles', the diabolic spirit uttered no word for three days. Only on the fourth day, at 8 p.m., he spluttered: "I am here! I am in a fury!"

"Who are you?" asked the Sister.

"I am the lord of darkness!" he cried and imitated the cry of a calf about to be strangled.

When angry, the boy's features were dreadful to behold. He then recognized no one, not even his own mother. He tore his clothes to pieces and smashed everything near him, until he was overpowered. On receiving a garment, into which a blessed medal had been sewn, he made it his first business to tear away the lining and wrench out the sacred object. His deafness was so great that he failed to hear Monsieur le Superieur Stumpf firing some pistol shots near his ear. He watched the motion of the finger on the trigger, and then, even whilst the loud report was still echoing through the room, he cried: "He wants to shoot, but cannot manage it!"

One day, Monsieur le Superieur came from Strasbourg on a visit to St. Charles' Institute. He drove in a carriage in company of a parish priest. Thiebaut was drumming with his fingers on the window pane. No sooner did he perceive the visitors than he exclaimed, "Look! There comes the dungbeetle [*Dreckler*]! Wait! I am going to play him a trick!" A couple of seconds later, a wheel became detached from its axle and the visitors had to walk the rest of the way. To play nasty pranks, to torment and torture in every possible way the "two little dogs" [meaning the boys]: that was the demon's constant occupation. For four years the poor victims had to remain in this awful predicament.

Many people in the metropolis absolutely refused to believe in the diabolic possession and remained impervious even to the findings of the first official enquiry. After two more years, however, a second commission of investigation was formed. It meant the end of the long torture, and the liberation of the unfortunate boys. In May, 1868, Monsieur Brobeck and M. le Maire decided to take Thiebaut to Notre Dame des Ermites (Einsiedeln), in the hope of a cure in that place of pilgrimage. The journey was safely accomplished. Two Benedictine fathers kept the boy under close observation, until the reality of the possession became clear to them. Father Nepomuk said over him, three times, but without success, the liturgical prayers of exorcism. He then advised to pilgrims to go to the Bishop with the request that that prelate would take authoritative steps towards the liberation of the children from their ghastly affliction. The Capuchin fathers of Dornach had already given the same advice.

An officer of an African regiment quartered at Mulhouse, who was very fond of sensational sights, came once to visit the possessed boys. As soon as they saw him, they roused his conscience with such a thorough examination in classical French, that he was overcome and rushed away terrified. It was the occasion of his resuming religious duties after long neglect, and being sincerely converted. A similar experience befell a school inspector of Mulhouse, and two gentlemen of the town. The frightful sight of effects of diabolic malignity in the boy was the occasion of making good Christians of them all.

On Tuesday morning, March 3, 1868, Monsieur Burner, the father of the boys, went to market. In the outskirts of the city he met a little man, a wandering needle-and-thread merchant known to everyone in the district. This man assailed Burner with bitter reproaches. "You are," he pried, "the cause of your children's misfortune! You befoul them with *occultism*!" Burner defended himself as best he could, but was unable to convince his adversary. When he returned home, the boy shouted at him from a distance: "What a nice scene the little merchant made with you! He has reproached you with playing mysterious games with your boys!"

"Was he also one of 'your own'?" asked the father.

"Yes!" replied the demon, through the boy's mouth. "Yes! Already I have him in my net!"

"Then," replied Burner, "I will say one *Pater noster* for the poor man's deliverance, and will forget his insolence to me!" Hearing this prayer, the devilish being exclaimed, "Alas! Now my net is being torn! The man eludes me!"

On a fast-day, the demon caused the boy to shout most loudly for meat, contrary to Church regulations. In so doing, he used the French language: "*Va me chercher de la viande, ou je sons par la fenêtre.*" On other days, it never came into his head to ask for meat!

He supremely hated prayer. One day, Monsieur Tresch brought with him an old book of the year 1648, containing some powerful prayers against evil spirits. He had scarcely opened it, when he was simply overwhelmed with every opprobrious epithet that can be imagined. "Very well!" said the *Maire*. "You begin, and I continue!" The boys jumped on their bed, crying: "You always carry with you these *old dirty leaves*!" and Thiebaut added: "You turn me into a lunatic! I cannot listen to you any more! I become mad and I ought to be taken to Stephansfeld!" (the asylum). Then they seemed about to leap at the *Maire* with the purpose of biting and scratching him. He held forth his hand and challenged them to strike it if they dared. But, although they tried to do so, their blows fell right and left ineffectively!

On other occasions they rarely succeeded in their evil designs against opponents. It happened that Monsieur l'Abbé Schrantzer, who argued against the demon, received a scratch-wound from Thiebaut. This priest took no heed of the insignificant injury, which ached but little. On the second day, however, his finger was noticeably swollen and very painful. He took fright and bathed the wound in holy water. The next day, all pain was gone, as was also every trace of the scratch!

Another time, the boy took the chair and flung it against the Abbé, whose head escaped by a mere inch or so. The Abbé, seeing him about to repeat the assault, touched the boy's hand with holy water. This sufficed! The boy released hold of the chair, and betook himself, grunting and growling, into a corner.

Bishop Stumpf

Rector Hausser
(Former Chaplain of St. Charles's).

M. le Vicaire Général,
Freyburger.

Monsieur le Député,
Ignace Spies

St. Charles's, Schiltigheim.

General View of Illfurt.

Cemetery Chapel, Illfurt.

CHAPTER X
SATAN'S CONFESSIONS

Monsieur Martinot mentions, in one of his letters, how the worthy *Maire* of Illfurt, extracted from the possessed boy a declaration as to which religion is true. "Thou knowest it!" said the devilish inhabitant of the boy's body. "Thy religion is the only true one! All others are false!"

"But how is it," asked Monsieur Tresch, "that you *acknowledge* such a fact?"

"I am forced to it by the Three who are above [the Holy Trinity]" said the demon, adding: "I must also inform you that we have no power whatever — we demons — over people who think and act as you do. We are powerless against those who confess their sins with sorrow in their heart and receive worthily the body of Christ. We can do nothing against those who invoke the Great Lady to whom also *we* owe our misfortune. [See Genesis 3:15]. We cannot harm the sincere followers of the great Teacher whom we hate: that is, the people who are loyally devoted to "*dem Voter aller Hunde* [the father of all the dogs, abusive name for the Pope!], and are devout members of *dem grossem-Schweinestall* [the demon's term for the Church Catholic]."

Questioned by Monsieur Martinot about his name, "My name," he said, "and thine, are as well known to me as to thee; but I have my reasons for refusing to say what it is. If you were a Jew," he added, "I'd answer in all languages!" Next day, Monsieur Tresch asked the spirit why he was so headstrong and rude with the two gentlemen from Selestat. "I cannot," was the reply, "stand *that 'Spitz,'* nor endure the other one. The *man who lives in chat town but is not a native of it* [Monsieur Martinot was born in the department de la Meurthe] prays too much! What he has, he gives to the poor, retaining for himself scarcely a few rags! He knocks at the door of the rich to find relief for the poor. I cannot bear him! Never again mention his name to me!"

To Monsieur Tresch the spirit was equally rude. One day he compared him to a great far spreading branch. "But you are a skinflint! a starveling!" he added. "You give me nothing: not even your potato peelings! You bestow all on *the Great Lady and her dog*! Even in your home you keep *the Great Dame with her little dog on her lap*!"

"Where is she placed?" he was asked. "Over the door? Yes; but that is not the one you fear?"

"No," answered the fiend; "but the one you keep in your little box: the *one with the little dog on the lap*!" The statuette to which the spirit undoubtedly referred was a gift from the Maire's aunt from St. Pilt, and a great object of veneration to him.

One Sunday morning, whilst the church bell tolled the sacred mysteries on the altar, Satan flew into a veritable frenzy. "Wait," said the nursing-Sister to him. "The time is near when you will have to depart! Can I not expel you myself?"

"Your nose is too short for that!" jeered the demon.

"Who can do it, then?" enquired the Sister. "Charles Brey," was the reply. The fiend possessing Thiebaut also declared that he would be defeated "in the presence of twelve persons," and that "the little dog" [Thiebaut] would then recover the sense of hearing: "but," added the evil one, "I shall put up a good defence!" Our narrative will show how stout a resistance he actually did offer to the exorcist who expelled him from his victim and that this event did take place in the presence of twelve witnesses!

A holy priest, an ex-chaplain of St. Charles', came purposely to Schiltigheim on a visit to the boys. Entering the room, he uttered the Latin greeting, "*In nomine Jesu omne genuflectatur*": ["In the name of Jesus let every knee bent in heaven, on earth, and under the earth."] Immediately, the possessed boy collapsed in a heap. Then he began to moan and cry and, with a howl, crawled under the bed.

The priest repeated the same words, and ordered the boy to approach.

On receiving a refusal, the priest put holy water under the bedstead. The boy crept out of the hiding place, turned whimperingly on the floor, and then hastened to a corner as far away from the priest as possible.

Mdselle. Marie Spies, sister of Monsieur Spies, called one day and touched one of the boys with a finger on which she wore a blessed medal of St. Hubert. "Cease!" cried the possessed boy. "You have *fire* on you! You burn me" Then he grinned, "The bombs did not damage thy hut. Thou hast the Great Lady in it! (He alluded to the siege of Selestat in 1814, during which the house of the Spies family remained intact. The same house was also unharmed in the war of 1870).

CHAPTER XI
THE EPISCOPAL COMMISSION

After the lapse of nearly five years, the diocesan authorities took the case in hand. His lordship, Bishop Raess, remained always amongst the most sceptical. Not until the report of his own episcopal commission of enquiry was issued did he become convinced of the fact of diabolic possession. At the instance of the Dean of Altkirch, he ordered a special ecclesiastical investigation. For this purpose, he sent, on April 13, 1869, to Illfurt, three theologians: Monsieur Stumpf, Superior of the Great Seminary; Monsieur Freyburger, Dean of Ensisheim; and Monsieur Sester, rector of Mulhouse.

The parish-priest of the village being temporarily absent, it was the *Maire*, Monsieur ,Tresch, who received these gentlemen, and accompanied them to the Burner family. There they met the mother and the two boys. The diabolic possessor had already predicted their arrival, and had even named who they would be. "The man who comes from Strasbourg harms me most!" he added. "He is sent here by *the cleric with the big cap* [mitre; he alluded to the Bishop]; but I shall play the fool with him and with the others."

The enquiry lasted all the morning. It quite convinced the commission of the true nature of the astounding affliction. The boys became intensely excited. On being touched with a medal of the Blessed Virgin, Thiebaut hid himself under the bed and Joseph leapt out of the window.

The reverend gentlemen put into written form every possible detail of evidence available. Witnesses were heard, whose statements tallied with the investigators' own observations. At last, the commission drew up its report and forwarded it to Strasbourg.

Monsieur le Superieur Stumpf advised the bringing over of the boys to a convent in the episcopal city, where the exorcism could take place. This plan was in agreement with the ideas of Monsieur Spitz, who proposed, for this purpose, the Orphanage of St. Charles, near Schiltigheim, one of the institutions which belonged to the Convent of All Saints. The Vicar-General, Msgr. Marula, expressed the wish of having the elder boy removed first. This was agreed to and Thiebaut was taken to the Orphanage. There he remained for five weeks, tended by the nuns, until the time of his deliverance.

A previous enquiry was to have taken place, but failed to materialize, owing to peculiar circumstances. This fact was well known to the evil spirit. In the presence of Messieurs Spies and Martinot, Monsieur Tresch asked the elder boy, during a crisis, "Tell me: where have you been today?"

"Oh!" replied the demon, speaking by medium of the boy. "Oh, I have not been wasting my time! I was today at Strasbourg!"

"And what were you doing there?"

"I have been playing the fool on five priests!"

"How?"

"I donned a cassock, and succeeded in putting them off the track! Soon after, these gentlemen were informed that an enquiry was to have taken place at the instance of the ecclesiastical authorities. But the task was not at all to the liking, they were also told, of the priest who was entrusted with it. This latter came to Illfurt, but saw neither parents nor boys. He did not even cross the threshold of the house! The enquiry fell through, and the deadly malignity of the possessing fiend was thereby strengthened!"

The most prominent man among the sceptics was the schoolmaster of Illfurt. During school hours, he poured ridicule on the events in the Burner family, and ended by saying, "The devil, in fact, does not exist!" Shortly afterwards, he went with two of his children to his native village, in the neighbourhood of Colmar, to settle some private affairs. On the Champ de Mars of this town, he saw a company of soldiers drilling.

Posting himself in front of these, "I am Napoleon!" he shouted: "Napoleon, the Emperor of the French!" On saying this, he took a paper, went straight up to the commanding officer and acted as though about to confer a military decoration upon him. He had suddenly become mad! He was taken to the Hospital, and then to Stephansfeld lunatic asylum. The evil spirit had foretold this incident also! It had done so with mockery and laughter.

A great number of conversions, however, resulted from this striking case of lunacy. Many people recovered their long lost religious fervour. One woman knocked at the door of the Redemptorist monastery at Landser and expressed a desire to make a general confession. "I saw the poor children," she said, "and the devil seemed to take a great delight in me. I am anxious about the state of my soul."

A brigadier of the military police, who long ago had lost his faith through reading evil books, paid casual visits, with Monsieur Tresch, to the Burner family. Each time he called, the possessing spirit was quiet and did not reveal himself. The man, therefore, was inclined to treat the matter as humbug. He happened, however, to come one day, accompanied by the *Maire*, whilst a crisis of particular violence was in progress.

The sight of so appalling a scene was enough to convince the unbeliever and to shake him to the depths of his being. "I am going to turn over a new leaf!" he told his wife. "I am going to become a fervent Christian!" He kept his word. He was present at divine service as often as his duty allowed and received the Sacraments every month.

CHAPTER XII
A SCENE AT ST. CHARLES'

In an interesting message to his parents at Ribeauville, dated October 5, 1869, Monsieur Charles Andre, the gardener of St. Charles', describes the following impressive scene, of which he himself was an eye and ear-witness. "On Saturday, Sister Damase," he said, "asked me to take Thiebaut to the chapel, exerting, if necessary, force to that end. I thought it an easy task. What an error I had made! The fourteen-year-old boy was secured and held fast by me. The Sisters blindfolded him, so as to prevent him from seeing where we were going. I turned my face towards the chapel. Scarcely, however, had we advanced a step in that direction, than the boy, who until then had been quiet, became furious and refused to budge. I lifted him up to carry him. He was very heavy and I had to use all my strength to master him. We made our way to the chapel as best we could, half-carrying, half-dragging, the unfortunate Thiebaut. The only noise he made was that of a howling bulldog. The Sisters offered assistance and took the boy by his feet, but he slung his legs apart and threw the Sisters off. At the step of the chapel, he was raging, whining, and twisted about in my arms like a snake. Suddenly, he twisted his legs round mine so strongly that nobody could move them. I was fastened as with iron chains, and fell side ways against the chapel wall. My shirt was wet with sweat and my breath became very difficult. After a little rest, I laboured up the steps with my human burden. I came to the chapel door. It had been opened and I stood at the entrance. On a sudden, the boy was struck as by lightning. He simply collapsed in my arms! He seemed as though dead! Froth covered his mouth! His deep-sunk eyes were fast shut! He showed no faintest sign of life I dragged him as far as the centre of the chapel, where we both fell on the floor. For two minutes, the boy remained silent like a corpse. Then there came a sudden inrush of life, and the boy howled like a ravening dog. 'Away!' he howled. 'Away with this filth! Let me get out of this pigsty!' He raved. A yellow foam gathered on his lips. I wanted to get a good view of his eyes and, for that purpose, I bent over the body. As a reward of my curiosity, he blew the horrible froth into my face. He twisted round like a crushed worm. His howling was terrifying beyond expression. He tried to crawl back to the chapel door, but his movements were now very slow. His weakness caused him to have some strange convulsive movements. It was all horribly gruesome and the darkness of the night increased our terror. After half an hour, I pulled the boy out of the building. Scarcely had the door closed behind him, than he rose and walked! I took him by the arm and led him back to his room. This scene made a deep impression upon us all. We were speechless but full of thought, and we were struck with amazement."

"The boy is deaf. This deafness has been tested in all kinds of ways. He speaks very little during the day, and then like a child, with a pure, sweet voice. As soon, however, as the evil spirit begins to speak through him, his tone becomes strong, like that of a powerful bass voice. It becomes husky and difficult to understand. He seeems to be indifferent to his surroundings. He walks along strangely, like a maniac, never fixing his eyes on a child under six or seven years: never touching any such innocents! Never does he gaze on a religious picture, but he delights in beholding animals: Spiders and toads are his darlings! He is often on the look out for such vermin, and for insects, playing with them, causing them to run up his hands. He would then delight in tearing their legs from their bodies.

'He eats, as a rule, like an ordinary human being, but at times he turns into a horrible glutton. For example, a little while ago he emptied a big basketful of apples, and devoured them to the last one!"

"The Sister brings him food: but let her sprinkle it with holy water, or touch it with a blessed medal! Although it had been done in the kitchen, right out of his sight, he would infallibly know of it! He then will approach the dish, look at it, and say, 'I am not hungry! There is filth in this food!' or, 'This food is poisoned!'

"In no circumstances will he touch such food, but always waits for another helping! (The same thing happens with liquids. He can never be induced to touch them if any holy water has been put into them, or if any pious object has been brought into contact with them! His favourite expression for a church is '*Saustall!*' — 'pigsty'. For holy-water he uses the terms '*Sauwasser,*' or '*Dreckwasser*' (filth water). He calls priests 'Black-cowls,' or 'Blackguards.' In his vocabulary, the religious sisters were 'patients all covered over with dirt.' Catholics he described as 'dung-beetles.' The poor afflicted boys themselves were 'his pups.' He had, however, words of praise for Freemasons and rebellious Christians! Such, he maintained, were 'fine people. They suit us!' cried the diabolic spirit; 'they are the protagonists of liberty!' He always spoke of them with the greatest delight. 'They render us, gentlemen, great service!' he cried. (He always called himself a 'gentleman,' and the devils he designated as his `masters'). 'They [the Freemasons and disobedient Christians] spare us a lot of trouble!' he screeched; 'they bring many people under our sway, whereas the *filthy dung-beetles* and the *blackcowls* [*die Dreckler und Schwarzkutten*] spoil much of our valuable work, give us great trouble and take away from us many souls!"

"When the evil spirit speaks through the mouth of the boy, he always casts him into a kind of trance. The body on such occasions appears lifeless. The boy's features are rather handsome, but his face is pale and melancholic. He lives, and walks about, like a person labouring under the burden of a heavy cross."

CHAPTER XIII
THIEBAUT'S DELIVERANCE

As already stated, the elder boy, Thiebaut, was, at the beginning of September, 1869, taken to the orphanage of St. Charles, near Schiltigheim. His unhappy mother accompanied him. In the Institute, a new and very complete investigation was ordered by his lordship the Bishop, under the supervision of the Vicar-General, Msgr. Rapp, l'Abbé Stumpf, president of the seminary, and Father Eicher, the Superior of the members of the Society of Jesus in Strasbourg. At the same time, Monsieur l'Aumomer Hausser, together with a Strasbourg theologian, l'Abbé Schrantzer, kept the boy systematically and closely under the most careful observation.

In outward appearance the boy was very strange. He was very thin and pale and left the impression of a child who had outgrown his years. In his big black eyes lurked something unsteady — something insecure, conveying a strange sensation to those who beheld him. His features were tired and drawn, like a patient's after a long illness.

Most of the time, he remained quiet, and whiled away the hours with games or with walks in the yard. He conversed with visitors in perfectly correct French and sometimes answered in Latin: but never himself began in the latter tongue.

The chapel, however, was an object of terror to him. It was useless to blindfold him or to lead him in all directions through corridors! As soon as he came into the vicinity of the church, he would struggle with all his strength and refuse to go any further. His resistance was always punctuated with unnatural yells. When forced into the sacred building, he collapsed like a log and his features took on a horrible appearance. Besprinkled with holy-water, he would wriggle like a worm under a foot. Quietude returned only when he was taken out of the chapel.

On October 3, a carriage stood ready in the yard of the Orphanage to fetch froin Strasbourg the reverend president of the Seminary, the reverend Mother General, and the reverend Father, who was to be exorcist.

All was ready for the departure, when Monsieur l'Abbé Schrantzer handed to the coachman a blessed medal of St. Benedict. The yard is bisected by a building and Thiebaut, walking on the other side, could have had no possible means of knowing this incident.

At 2 o'clock, the reverend gentlemen arrived from the City and immediately began the process of exorcism. The boy was forcibly taken into the chapel, where he was held fast by the Abbés Schrantzer and Hausser, assisted by the gardener, Monsieur Andre. He stood on a carpet before the communion rails, with his face turned towards the tabernacle. His colour recalled that of a man under a fever. From his lips was gushing a thick froth, which flowed down on to the floor.

The possessed boy turned and wriggled, as though seated on a glowing furnace. Often he turned his face towards the door. Whenever the Abbé Schrantzer touched his chest with a crucifix, it was seen to arch itself and swell like a balloon.

Now began the ceremonies of exorcism. Father Souquat, who had been entrusted by the bishop with this difficult task, at first hesitated, not altogether convinced of its being an actual case of real possession, he having come, until then, only slightly into contact with the poor sufferer.

"Go away from here!" shouted the Satanic spirit, through the mouth of the boy. "Clear off, you *Dreckler!*" In the presence of five priests — the archpriest Spitz, President Stumpf, Professor Rosse, Chaplain Hausser, and Abbé Schrantzer, — also of six nuns and the mother of the poor boy, Father Souquat began to recite the Litany of All Saints.

At the words, "Holy Mary, pray for us," the Satanic being howled dreadfully: "Out of this *Saustall*, you *Stinker*!"

"I will not!" In this wise he shouted each time a great Saint was invoked, and especially when they said, "All ye holy angels and archangels, pray for us."

When the reverend father came to the words, "From the snares of the devil, deliver us, O Lord," the afflicted boy shook, and trembled in all his limbs. His dreadful yell rent the air. He turned and twisted with such a force that the two priests and the gardener could scarcely hold him with their united efforts.

After the recitation of the Litany, Father Souquat faced the boy and said over him the prayers prescribed in the Ritual. The possessed cried incessantly, "Away with you, foul one! Out of this '*Saustall!*'" On hearing the words, "Glory be to the Father, to the Son, and to the Holy Spirit."

"*I will not!*" he cried (v.d.i give glory to the blessed Trinity).

Before reading the Gospel of St. John, the priest made the sign of the cross, on the victim's forehead, lips and breast. The boy replied by growling like a bull-dog and actually snapping at him, as for a bite. The exorcist then questioned him, speaking in German, "You spirit of darkness, crushed serpent, I, a priest of the Lord, command thee, in His almighty name, to tell me who thou art!"

"What's that to thee, thou *stinkpot*? I tell it to whom I like!" snarled the evil one.

"This," continued the priest, "is just a repetition of thy old proud behaviour, and thy defiant language before thy Creator at the fateful hour of thy expulsion from Heaven. But I command thee — *Begone, Satan*! Leave this church: for thou belongest not to the House of God! Thy home is in the darkness of hell!"

"But *I will not!*" grinned the demon. "My time is not yet come!" After three hours of prayers and holy efforts, the exorcist was still resisted by the fiend.

Father Souquat was bathed in sweat; tired, but not dismayed, he gave up his zealous endeavours and took leave of his friends, promising to go on with the work of expulsion another day. The boy was removed from the chapel and quietened down at once.

That same evening, the Abbé Schrantzer had a conversation with him. "You have done well," the boy said, "to give 'a little piece of tin' to him!"

"To whom?" asked the Abbé.

"Surely, to the coachman!"

"How can you know this and what would you have done otherwise?" asked the Abbé, remembering the incident (utterly unknown to the boy) of the giving of the medal of St. Benedict to the coachman.

"I would have knocked down men, horses and carriage!" replied the demon, "I was galloping at the side of the animals!"

"But we have been a great worry to you in the chapel, haven't we?" said the Abbé. "Do you know the priest who has blessed you?"

"Oh, yes, I do!" answered the hellish foe. "He has already once expelled one of our masters!" It was a fact that Father Souquat, years before, when in Germany, had expelled a devil from a house. How could the boy have known of this exorcism through any natural means? This conversation was reported to Father Souquat and absolutely convinced him that it was a true case of diabolic possession.

On the next day (Monday), the reverend gentlemen returned from the city and the exorcist resumed his task. The boy was put into a straight jacket and tied on to a red armchair. The possessing devil raged more dreadfully than ever.

The chair, with the boy on it, was raised into the air and his three guards were thrown right and left by invisible bands. The roaring of the devilish spirit was earsplitting and the froth, flowing from the boy's mouth, was an object of horror not soon to be forgotten.

When, after about two hours, the reverend father had come to the end of the liturgical prayers, he rose and addressed the demon: "Now, impure spirit, thy time is at hand! I order thee, in the name of the Catholic Church, in the name of God, and in my own name as his priest, to tell me how many you are!" The same sound and the same answer, as before, came: "This has nothing to do with thee, foul one!" growled the fiend.

"This is," replied the priest, "just the proud tone thou indulgest in here on earth and which resounds in hell! Thy home is in the abyss of darkness, not in the abode of light! Impure Satan, depart into hell!"

"I will not go there!" replied the demon. "I want to lodge in another place!"

"I adjure thee," cried the priest, once more, "to tell me how many you are!"

"We are," answered Satan, "two only."

"What," continued the priest, "is thy name?"

"Oribas."

"And the other one's name,"

"Ypès."

"Unclean spirits, I order you," cried the priest, "to leave the house of God!"

"You have nothing to do in it!"

"Spirits of perdition, depart from here!",said the priest. I command it in the name of the Blessed Sacrament!"

"*I will not*!" growled the master of evil. "Skunk, thou hast no power over me! My hour has not yet struck!" The priest trembled all over his body and a heavy sweat ran down his face. His emotions were no less terrible than the awe and horror which overwhelmed all the onlookers.

But the brave priest did not lose his courage nor his trust in God. Again he commenced his holy struggle with Satan. He took a crucifix and placed it before the boy's eyes. "Thou miserable spirit!" he cried. "Thou darest not even behold this image! Thou turnest thy face away in order not to see it! Thou biddest defiance to the priest of God! I command thee to leave God's temple and to sink into hell, which is prepared for thee!"

"*I will not*!" the demon groaned. "It is not good to be there!"

"Hadst thou been obedient to thy Maker, thou wouldst not be in thy state of misery," replied the priest. "Thy *pride* has brought about thy fall and thy misfortune! Thou art a spirit of darkness ;

depart, therefore, from the light and return into the darkness assigned to thee!"

Again the Satanic being exclaimed: "My time has not come yet! *I will not go!*" On this, the priest took a candle which had been blessed by the Pope and said: "Thou proud Satan, I place this candle on thy head! to light thee on thy way to hell! This is the light of the Catholic Church and thou art a spirit of darkness! Go back to hell and remain with those wicked spirits with whom thou art associated!"

"*I'll stay here!*" answered the demon. "Here, I am comfortable! In hell, misery reigns, and wretchedness!"

At last, Father Souquat raised up a statue of Our Lady, saying, "Behold an image of the Blessed Virgin Mary! She is again going to crush thy head! She must mark thee again and write, with her name, the holy name of Jesus on thy breast! that they burn thee for ever! Still thou offerest resistance! I have ordered thy departure in the name of our Lord Jesus Christ, in the name of the Catholic Church and in the names of our holy father the Pope and of the most blessed Sacrament! Thou heedest not the voice of the priest. *Now*, therefore, it is the Mother of God who orders thee away! *She it is who forces thee to leave this boy!* Unclean spirit, disappear before the face of the Immaculate Conception! She commands! Thou must obey! thou must depart!"

Whilst this injunction was being made, all the onlookers recited the *Memorare*. Most solemn was this moment! Suddenly, a most horrible yell from the fiend's deep bass voice filled with echoes the sacred place: "Now I must yield!" cried the demon.

Once more the boy turned and twisted like a crushed serpent. A gentle cracking was observed in the juvenile body. The boy stretched himself, lengthened out and collapsed like a corpse. *The devil had left him*!

It had been an awe-inspiring sight, full of horror to all the witnesses. Only a moment ago, the fiercest rage, a face writhing in fury, the most defiant answers! Now, Thiebaut lies still for a whole hour in a deep sleep. He is freed! No longer does he fly from holy objects! He allows himself to be carried gently back into his room. There he wakes up, after a while, rubs his eyes and looks amazed at the many unknown persons surrounding him!

"Do you know me?" asked the Abbé Schrantzer.

"No; I do not," answered the boy.

A cry of joy is uttered by his mother. Her Thiebaut has recovered his sense of hearing! and he is freed from the hellish spirit! All of them thank God, who has given His Church such power over Hell! Full of gladness, the happy mother returns to Illfurt with Thiebaut. She has the firm hope of witnessing, in the near future, the freeing of her second son, Joseph.

This trust was to be realized on the twenty-seventh day of the same month.

CHAPTER XIV
JOSEPH ALSO IS DELIVERED

Returned once more to his father's house, Thiebaut was bright and happy; but, of all that had happened during the fateful years of his bondage, he had not the least recollection. He did not even recognize the Abbé Brey, his parish priest, nor could he remember ever having seen the new municipal buildings. He had brought from Strasbourg some medals for his brother Joseph. When, however, he made the offer of them, that boy threw them on the floor and said, "Keep that stuff for yourself! I do not want it!"

This behaviour amazed Thiebaut (who, of course we must bear in mind, knew nothing whatever, in his healed state, of the diabolic possession either of himself or of his brother, and had no idea that anything at all was the matter with Joseph). Thiebaut said to his mother, "Has Joseph become mad?" Of course, great care was taken not to divulge to him the secret cause of his brother's action.

On Wednesday evening, the possessed boy Joseph shouted: "My two comrades [Oribas and Ypès, the devils who had possessed Thiebaut] are cowards! Now, I am the master! I am the strongest!

I shall not depart for another six years! I am not afraid of clerics!"
"Are you then so powerful " asked Monsieur Tresch, who was present.

"Certainly I am!" he replied. "I feel comfortable and shall stay here! I slip into a nest and leave it when I like!"

Meanwhile, the Abbé Brey, the parish priest, had craved his Bishop's permission to attempt exorcism. The condition of the hapless Joseph grew indeed worse day by day.

Thiebaut, on the other hand, daily frequented school and church and resumed the Sacraments. He was the same boy as before the diabolic affliction. He remembered nothing of that long calamity. He was as though he had passed all that time in sleep!

At last, the parish priest received authorisation, from his Bishop, to attempt the exorcism of Joseph and he proceeded to the ceremony on October 27. Very early that morning, Joseph was taken to the cemetery chapel, a quarter of an hour's walk from Illfurt. The affair was kept secret, so as to avoid a crowd. Only a few witnesses were invited:" Professor Lachemann, of St. Hippolyte, Monsieur Ignace Spies of Selestat, Monsieur Martinot, and Monsieur Tresch. The boy's parents, the schoolmaster, and Monsieur Frindel, the stationmaster, completed the company.

When, at 6 a.m., Mass began, the boy became very noisy with his feet. He fidgeted about, so that his hands and feet had to be a manacled. At the *Introibo*, he managed to kick his legs free and flung the straps at the feet of the celebrant priest. Then Monsieur Martinot bound him on to his lap. Now barking like a dog, now grunting like a pig, now emitting, in a hoarse voice, inarticulate sounds, he remained, however (to everybody's amazement) quite motionless from the moment of the *Sanctus* and until the end of the Mass.

The priest, having put aside the sacred vestments, knelt, with surplice and violet stole, at the foot of the altar and began the prayers of exorcism: the Litany of All Saints and some forms of adjuration. Then he approached the possessed boy and ordered him to reveal the number of the spirits haunting him.

"You have no business to know this!" replied the afflicted child. The priest reiterated his command, and file child replied, dryly: "*Ypès!*" More than this could not be extracted from him.

During the reading of St. John's Gospel, the boy began to cast insults at the parish priest, shouting, under the influence of the devil possessing him, "*I shall not depart!*" During three successive hours the exorcist took all conceivable pains in his fight for the boy's liberty. *Now*, he placed holy relics on his head; *then* he put a blessed paschal candle between his arms; *again*, he sprinkled holy water over him, using meanwhile the most powerful formulae for expelling devils. Always, however, the demon groaned, "I go not away! I will not!" Those present began to feel discouraged. But the good pastor, although tired to death, exhorted them to persevere in hope. They said the Rosary.

Monsieur Tresch, who had held the boy all the time, delivered him over to the care of Professor Lachemann. When this was done, the boy howled: "Oh, *you* are here also, you *flatnose!*" The priest had come back from the altar, on the steps of which he had said a fervent prayer and promised a Novena. Turning himself towards the afflicted boy, "I adjure thee, Satan," he said, "in the name of the Immaculate Mother of Christ, to depart from this child!" A strong sound full of rage, was heard "Must this one also come, leaning on the Great Lady! Now I must leave him!"

An indescribable emotion gripped the witnesses of this drama. They were all convinced that the hour of liberation was at hand. Again the Abbé Brey repeated this adjuration. "I must yield now!" growled the Satanic one. "I will enter into a herd of pigs!"'

"Into *hell!*" commanded the man of God. The same words of adjuration resounded now for the third time.

"Let me go into a flock of geese!" pleaded the fiend.

"*Into hell!*" was the fiercely repeated reply, "I know not the way thither!" groaned the demon. "I'll take my lodgment in a sheep flock!"

For the last time came the categorical command: "*To hell!*" With a terrible yell, "Now I am forced to leave!" the boy stretched out his limbs, turned in various directions, puffed up his cheeks, and made a last convulsive movement. Then he lay silent and motionless.

He was unstrapped. His arms fell flat, and his head dropped

backwards. After a pause, he raised his arms and stretched them out like a man awakening from a deep slumber. Then he opened his eyes: which had been closed during the whole ceremony. He looked round in amazement to find himself in a church, with strange people around him!

The onlookers were deeply affected. With grateful hearts they recited the *Te Deum*, the Litany of Loreto, the *Salve Regina*, and other prayers, which were often interrupted by loud sobbing.

The Abbé Brey was often obliged to pause, tears of gratitude dimming his eyes, and emotion choking his voice.

How joyful was Joseph's return to his paternal home! Everyone from near and far admired the power of our Lady, who on this solemn occasion had overthrown once more the hellish dragon!

CHAPTER XV
VICTORY OF CHRIST'S MOTHER

When one day, reader, you come (as it is to be hoped you will) on a visit to Illfurt, you will see a beautiful monument facing the former Burner house. It is a statue of the Immaculate Conception, gilt, of cast-iron, standing on a pillar of stone. This monument is 30 feet high and towers above all the surrounding buidings. On its plinth is a Latin inscription: "*In memoriam perpetuam liberationis duorum possessorum Theobaldi et Iosephi Burner, obtentae per intercessionem Beatae Mariae Virginis Immacalatae, Anno Domini 1869*": ("In everlasting memory of the liberation of the two possessed boys, Thiebaut and Joseph Burner, obtained through the prayers of the Blessed Virgin, Mary Immaculate, in the year 1869").

The good pastor, Abbé Brey, could not help paying this tribute of gratitude to the heavenly Mother and his parishioners and other devout lovers of our Lady were only too eager to contribute their mite towards the erection of this noble column.

It was indeed most striking, that at Schiltigheim, as well as at Illfurt, the Immaculate Virgin had overcome the Prince of

Darkness and again had crushed the serpent's head! All other forms of exorcism remained without result until Satan had to yield to the power of the prayers of the "Great Lady"! Into her hands the Almighty had placed victory, as in the realms of eternity He had bestowed it once upon Michael the Archangel in his fateful struggle with Lucifer. Mary is the potent Lady, the terror of hell! To her must yield all the powers of darkness! To her be honour, glory and gratitude throughout eternity!

And now you may ask, dear reader, "Why the appalling possession of these pitiful children? Who had sinned, the parents, or they themselves?"

Read chapter IX of St. John's Gospel, which mentions the miraculous healing of the man born blind. There you find the answer to your query. In this case also, God allowed the great affliction in order to show forth His works and to recall to mind the all important truth of His Redemption.

Before the coming of the Saviour, Satan in this world was almost lord and master. Almost everywhere had he set up his kingdom: the reign of unbelief, superstition and idolatry. He could truly claim the title, "Prince of this world!" Christ Himself called him by that name. Before dying on the cross, for the salvation of men, He said: "Now is the judgment of the world: now shall the prince of this world be cast out" (John 12:31). We understand these divine words to mean that, through faith in Christ, by His death and resurrection all men of good will shall be freed from the domination of Satan and shall be united with their Saviour, here in love and hereafter in everlasting bliss Christ Himself, when on earth, manifested His power over Satan by expelling him from those possessed whom He met in His journeys. This same Divine power He has left to His Apostles and His Church: "In My name you shall drive out devils": (Mark 16:17).

In His name the Apostles did this with wonderful success, and the Church has to the present day always exercised the same power of exorcism and with the same result as at Schiltigheim and Illfurt. No prince can boast such a power — no potentate, however great! — but it remains in the hands of the Catholic Church and its priests. To them alone has Christ entrusted this awful privilege.

Their word expels Satan, both from the souls and bodies of men. Bodily possession is, in our times, a rare event.

More frequent, alas, is Satan's ownership of the soul by its being in a state of mortal sin! Satan finds every advantage in not manifesting himself too frequently in tangible, bodily possessings, for they are always accompanied by such horrors that men turn from him in disgust and come back in penitence to God, as was the case at Illfurt. Satan now chooses rather to enter, secretly and in silence, into the human heart through deadly sin, and make his abode in that living temple. How much pain he takes, indefatigable, patient and cunning! With his seductive temptations he penetrates into the 'spiritual vitals of man, to separate him from his God, and to drag him, body and soul, into eternal misery! Once he takes possession of a heart, he robs it mercilessly of its rest and peace, of the merits of its good works, of God its Maker, and often, alas, finally of eternal happiness!

If, Christian reader, you had been at Illfurt during those years of real devilish visitation: if, like countless witnesses, you had seen with your own eyes the hair raising performances of the hellish spirits, would you, then, were it in your power to do otherwise — would you hug to your heart this loathsome and tyrannical foe? Would you choose to live, even if but for half an hour with this atrocious monster? Yet that is what you do as soon as you consent to a deliberate, mortal sin! When you do that, then one or more unclean spirits are certainly lodging in your soul! There they remain until you repent and until the powerful word of God's absolving priest drives the fiend from you.

Unfortunately, man, while alive in this world, does not realize the horrible burdensomeness of this possession of the soul by evil powers. Many live that unnatural life for weeks — maybe for years! One day, however, the mortal husk of the soul will fall into dust and upon the unforgiven soul will fall, alas, nameless woe!

If, already on earth, Satan deals, in the cruel way which we have described, with innocent children, how much more cruelly will he treat the damned! Them the anger of God will have placed within his power because in this mortal life they themselves chose his company and his domination! How dreadful beyond all expression must be this dwelling together with such hateful, infamous, godless and wicked wretches! How much we need to pray, with the pious Psalmist: "O Lord, abandon not to the beasts the souls that trust in Thee!" (Psalm 73:19). What reason we have for frequently repeating the liturgical invocation: "From the snares of the devil deliver us, O Lord!" May we remain true in the Christian faith, and keep grace in our hearts, and Satan shall not harm us, either in life or in eternity!

CHAPTER XVI
WORLDLY WISDOM AND PROFESSORIAL MISCONCEPTIONS

Against the fact of diabolical possession there was almost immediately raised a loud cry of opposition. The foremost to raise it were those who reject, *a priori*, the belief in the existence of evil spirits. They at once dispose of all such cases, together with liturgical exorcisms, with a disdainful smile or with a few pseudo-scientific phrases!

Most interesting is an essay on the Illfurt phenomena, by the learned noncatholic physiologist, Professor Hoppe. He had studied the case and had carefully read the booklet on it by Abbé Brey. He had also consulted ministers of religion of both denominations. He came to the conclusion that diabolic possession was something quite unintelligible to the human mind and he could not and would not contribute, he said, towards renewing what he called the idiotic belief in such a delusion!

"I frankly confess," he wrote, "that the exorcism performed

by the Catholic priests has indeed cured the two children ; but it was certainly not a case of devil-expulsion. It was simply a psychic healing of their diseased brain. I recognize in both children a hystericchoreatic derangement (*eine hysterisch-choreatische Verwirrtheit*), and I explain the case as follows: The whole soul – that is, the animated brain, in both patients, has itself imagined the devilishphantoms and has likewise been able to secure the healing and this was done by means of the brain-organism and of the psychic mechanism of the brain.

"The children exhibited a wonderful and immensely varied knowledge. That also was in them beforehand; it is nothing new or unheard of. The knowledge had merely been unobserved previously. Such knowledge was brought out by actual brain-excitation. Neither is there anything strange, now-a-days, in striking memory-phenomena. One needs not to consider them of diabolic origin. The belief in the lodging of a devil in the human brain is too ridiculous to be taken seriously by the present-day public."

With all respect to your great learning, honoured Professor, we take the liberty of calling your arguments very weak and unscientific. The problem you have to solve is that of children who are only eight or ten years old. What uncommon brains must theirs have been, to originate within themselves this devil-phantom. Yet brains without learning or experience — without the slightest knowledge of politics or history, what wonderful cerebral organizations theirs must have been, to enable children to speak fluently foreign languages they had never learned; to read the secret consciences of other men and to reveal to them their most hidden faults! Moreover, they spoke of scientific matters with such a clearness as cannot be surpassed by experts! They foretold, with accuracy afterwards verified by the event, things which were to happen in the future! They were (these boys) born in 1855 and 1857. Yet their memories recalled particulars of events that took place in certain Illfurt families during the Swedish War of 1639, and during the Revolution times of 1794!

To attribute such phenomena to a "hystericchoreatic derangement," and to explain them away with high-sounding words, is really "too ridiculous," learned Professor! It only shows to what depths of absurdity a learned man falls when he denies the supernatural at any price!

Naturally, the whole chorus of anti-religious newspapers of the day chimed in likewise! A specimen is found in the *Journal d'Altkirch* dated January 18, 1868: "In regard to devils we have become fairly sceptical, and, when mention is made of possessed people, we cannot help laughing?"

But superstition is a fact! It is with us! We cannot, then, raise our voices loudly enough against ideas which are fostered in the minds of the people for purposes which we do not wish to subject to closer examination... The two children, who were first treated by several doctors, were entrusted afterwards to the care of a Lady Hypnotizer (*von einer Schläferin*) (!). Then one of them was taken to a Capuchin monastery in our neighbourhood and subjected there to a very odd treatment. The devils, however, would not yield and the fuss, which was already widespread, increased. What was to be done? All remedies seemed to be exhausted, when the Government had the lucky thought to order an enquiry to be made on the spot by the brigadier of the police. "What was beyond the powers of science, mysticism, and exorcism, was easily done by a gentleman in galloons (*éin galonierter Herr*)! At his first visit the boys sweetened down; their mental condition became clarified ; their movements became natural, and the devil fled to all other devils! Happy journey!"

In this way a newspaper-scribbler writes history, not in Spain or in Holland, but only ten kilometres from Illfurt! Had he only dared to pay a personal visit to the children, what an interesting examination of conscience the devil would have made for him!

In another number of the same paper, dated February 1, 1868, another correspondent, with a pretence of wit, waxed sarcastic in the following article:

"*Le diable est a illfurt.* — Quelle riche moisson dès lors pour les chroniqueurs grands et petits! Les deux faibles créatures dont ii a choisi le corps pour lui servir de logement, sans être armées de la massue d'Hercule, font pâlir devant leurs exploits le Demi Dieu et ses travaux. Les crucifix, les amulettes attachés à leurs cou se pulvérisent avec fracas et accompagnement de flammes vertes et bleues et de parfums sulfurés: ils annoncent l'avenir, et, ô comble du miracle, sans cordes ni cloches, sonnent à toutes volées le glas funèbre de ceux, qui vont mourir! Et ce ne sont là, evidemment, que des, préludes: chaque jour apportera un prodige nouveau, jusqu 'à ce qu'il plaise à Satan, et puisse ce desir ne lui venir que bieri tard! de regagner pour un temps son domaine.

"Je ne rignore pas, les esprits foils poseront d'indisècrtes questions: ils demanderont pourquoi ces jeunes enfants, de préférence à tant d'autres qui y avaient incontestablement plus de titres, ont mérité le penible honneur de loger le Dieu cornu ; si on leur parle de cris rauques, d'yeux hagards, de convulsions et de spasmes, ile répoûldront par: hystérie, vapeurs on épilepsie et au lieu d'eau bénite ils recommandent des douches, une nourriture forte et même le régime si cher à MM. Fleurant, Purgon et Diatoirus: heureux s'ils ne prétendent que croyants et exorciseurs, exorciseurs, surtout, ont eux-mêmes un diable dansle corps, et le plus intraitable de tous, celui- de l'absurdité!"[1]

---

[1](TRANSLATION: "The devil is at Illfurt! What a rich harvest for newsmongers, great and small! In two weak creatures Satan has taken up his lodging! Without being armed with Hercules' club, they eclipse all the exploits of that half-god and his labours! Crucifixes and amulets, suspended round their neck, are being reduced to powder, with a great noise and accompaniment of green and blue flames and sulphurous perfumes! The children predict the future, and (0 zenith of miracle 1), without rope or bell they ring the funeral knell of those about to die! And these are evidently but preludes! Every day will bring a new miracle, until it pleases Satan (may his wish be long delayed!) to return for a time to his own domain! —But enlightened minds, as I am not unaware, are going to ask some indiscreet questions. They want to know why young children, in preference to many other people who undoubtedly had better titles to such honours, have deserved the painful glory of lodging the horned god. When they are told of hoarse cries, of haggard eyes, of convulsions, of spasms, they simply answer: Hysteria, vapours, epilepsy. Instead of holy-water, they recommend shower-baths, strong nourishing food, and even the regime so dear to Messrs. Fleurant, Purgon and Diatoirus. Happy if they do not argue that believers and exorcists (especially the latter) have not themselves a devil in their body, and that most refractory one of all: the devil of absurdity!"

We wish to show by such examples with what frivolous wantonness the unbelieving world judged these rare phenomena: a world which, of set purpose, disdained to subject them to a close and dignified enquiry. The Christian doctrine of hell and lost angels does not suit them ; consequently, they dispose of it with shrugs and cheap mockery!

Much more reserved were the doctors who had treated the children in the first period of the affliction, especially Dr. Krafft, Dr. Henry Weyer, Dr. Alfred Szertecki of Mulhouse! They found no natural explanation for the sickness, and dared not pass judgment on its mysterious nature. The Government physician of the canton, Dr. Levy, openly said to Abbé Brey that his science was of no use in this case, and that the Catholic Church had better remedies for it.

The news of the possession and liberation of the two boys spread as far as Paris. The great boulevard papers commented on it, and not always in a favourable sense. For example, Edmond About printed a correspondence in his *Opinion Nationale*, which represented the case as mere humbug, and represented that the children were still languishing in their state of misery. The *Industriel Alsacien* and the *Journal de Colmar* inserted this article in their columns.

Then the diocesan authorities had to take sides in refutation of this lie. The editors received, from the pen of the Vicar-General, Mgr. Rapp, the following rap on the nose:

"STRASBOURG, Jan. 9, 1870.
"To the Editor.
"Dear Sir,

You published in your number dated January 7 a correspondence from Strasbourg which calls for some corrections.

At Illfurt a small boy had for four years been afflicted by an extraordinary disease, of which the doctors were unable to determine the cause or nature. On repeated requests from the *Maire* of the parish, and from the parish priest, an enquiry was ordered by His Lordship the Bishop. It was decided that the child should be brought to the Orphanage at Schiltigheim, which is under the care of the Sisters of Charity. For some time, extraordinary facts, which it is superfluous to describe here, but which shall be published, with all necessary details, in a religious paper of Alsace, continued to occur, and the episcopal commission, of which nobody, except your correspondent, contests the wisdom and the authority, deemed it necessary to assign to these facts only a supernatural cause.

The Church has prayers for such cases, even when they are doubtful. These prayers have been said over the child, and he is completely cured.

Your correspondent says the contrary of the truth when he tells the public that the boy is still in his state of disease.

The mockeries and insults wherewith your correspondent has spiced his article may have gratified his readers. I have no concern with them.

It is only my intention to re-establish the facts, and I expect of your fairness that you will insert this letter in one of your early issues.

(Signed): RAPP, Vicar-General

LETTER FROM THIEBAUT BURNER TO RECTOR HAUSSER, FORMERLY CHAPLAIN OF ST. CHARLES'S ORPHANAGE
(Abbé Hausser, now retired, lives at Benfeld)

Whilst the younger boy, Joseph, at the beginning of his affliction, was only eight years old and could scarcely read and write, Thiebaut, his senior, had already made some progress at school, so that he was able (though imperfectly and not without mistakes) to read and write both French and German. When, however, a crisis came, during the diabolic possession, both children spoke several languages perfectly, and would talk to visitors for hours in faultless French.

It will interest our readers to glance over a letter written by Thiebaut, in the month of his liberation, to the chaplain Abbé Hausser. We reproduce it exactly as in the original, retaining all its quaint errors of spelling:

J.M.J.

ILLFURTH, le 31 October, 1869.
La sainte volonté de Dieu.

Monsieur Labé, aumonier.

J'ai l'honneur de vous montrer mes reconnaissances de tons les bienfait que j'ai reçu chez vous dans votre maison sacré par la grace de notre Seigneur Jésus Christ et sa très sainte Mere. C'est chez vous que j'ai a remercié mon bonheur de la deliverance de mes maux surnaturel, je suis très heureux maintenant, heureux comme Jamais: je me rejours maintenant avec mon Frère Josephe qui avait la même maladie comme moi et qui est guéris depuis le 27 Octobre par notre cher Monsieur le Curé et anjourd' hui dimanche nous avons célébre l'actions de grace avec tout le monde a l'Eglise avec le Te Deum et les sonnes des gloches et benediction du sainte sacrament pour ce boneheur infini.
Maintenant nous allons à l'Eglise et à l'Ecole comme si nous aurions éte jamais malade mais je crois que nous avions eu une trole de maladie parce que nous nous rapelons nous à aucune souffrance, mais grace a Dieu encore une fois nos sommes guérie.
Je finix en Dieu et en me recommandant dans vos prières.

recevez mes respectueux Salutation,
THIEBAUD BURNER

et aussi bien des compliment pour la Mére Superieure et pour la soeur Damas un bonjour de mes Parents pour toutes les soeurs.[2]

---

[2]TRANSLATION:" Dear Chaplain,
I am much honoured in telling you my gratitude for all the favours I have received at your house through our Lord Jesus Christ and His most holy Mother. It is at your home that I had, with many thanks, the happiness of being freed from my supernatural evils. I am very happy now — more happy than ever, — and I rejoice with my brother Joseph, who has been cured of the same affliction, on 27th October, by our dear parish priest, and today (Sunday) all the people flocked to the church. We have all celebrated our solemn *Te Deum* for this happy favour, and

The reader may wonder what eventually became of the two boys. Both, died young. The death of Thiebaut occurred two years after his liberation from the bonds of possession: namely, on April 3, 1871, when he was only sixteen years old. His brother Joseph found work at Zillisheim, and died there in 1882, at the age of twenty-five. The parish-priest, l'Abbé Brey, hastened to him and gave him the Last Sacraments.

---

have rung bells and had Benediction of the Blessed Sacrament. Now we go to church and school as though we had never been ill ; but I think it must have been a strange illness, because we cannot remember the slightest pain! But, thanks be to God, we are healed! I finish this letter with the thought of the Almighty, and I commend myself to your prayers. Receive my respectful salutations.

THIEBAUT BURNER.

(And also kind regards to the rev. Mother Superior and to Sister Damase, and a greeting from my parents to all the Sisters).

APPENDIX
REPORT OF EPISCOPAL COMMISSION

The following is a copy of the report of the Commission referred to in Chapter XI:

On Tuesday morning, April 13, 1869, at 10 o'clock, the three rev. gentlemen, Freyburger, Sester, and Stumpf, went straight to the presbytery. The parish priest, Abbé Brey, was unfortunately absent, but the *Maire*, Monsieur Tresch, quickly made his appearance and offered to show the way to the famous house of the Burners.

Not wishing to be seen by the children, who used often to sit near the window, the visitors went round the house and entered by the backdoor. The mother received them. She was a poor woman, forty years of age, and having an appearance of one suffering under great mental depression.

They found one boy only. He was sitting at a table, winding some reels of cotton into skeins. He was Thiebault. Joseph was hiding under a bed in the adjoining room. He offered – the most violent opposition to attempts to drag him from his seclusion and great efforts were needed before he could be drawn forth. He covered his face, and refused to look at anyone for ten minutes.

Monsieur Tresch took up a position on the threshold between the two rooms in order to prevent a possible escape. Thiebaut continued his work with the cotton reels. He is a handsome boy, between thirteen and fourteen years old, and completely deaf. His behaviour is modest and calm, his gaze is simple and sincere. His face is candid, but drawn and sad.

After a few moments, Mgr. Stumpf takes from his pocket a medal blessed by our holy father the Pope. He presents it to Joseph, whose age seems eleven years. He is a little rascal, full of sportive trickeries and very quick with his eyes. He keeps his head down. He seems to take no serious view of anything, but always to be ready for mischief: heedless, mocking, and taking no notice of the coaxings, or even of the gentle blows, with which Monsieur Tresch gratified him!

He had no sooner perceived the medal than he knocked it

from the hands of the visitor, and drew back as far as the wall, threatening to defend himself with kicks.

Monsieur Tresch picked up the medal and asked him to kiss it. The boy, however, struggled violently with him, grinning and writhing in a strange way.

All this time, Thiebaut remains silent, throwing only two or three indifferent glances at Joseph. Then Monsieur Stumpf presents him with the medal.

Immediately, Thiebaut thrust on one side the reels which had been interesting him so much, and drew back terrified. His face became scarlet.

As soon as he was left alone, he became quiet. He put the reels into a box, and sat modestly behind the table.

When Mess. Sester and Freyburger sat beside him, he reddened, became fidgetty, and went back to the wall. As soon as he was again left alone, he played with papers on the table, sharpened the nails of his fingers: but displayed constant anxiety, as one fearing a new attack.

Monsieur Tresch threw holy water on his fingers. Immediately he became violently agitated. He tried to run away, but finding no exit, he dropped on the floor to hide under the table. Monsieur Tresch, however, kept him back, and put him in front of the rev. visitors on another bench, at the foot of the bed, besides Mgr. Stumpf.

The boy, however, sought the other extremity of the bench. Now, the bed itself was hidden from view by a curtain of blue cotton hanging from the ceiling.

Monsieur Sester, unseen by the boy, sprinkled the inner side of the curtains with holy water. Behold the portent! — a great perturbation in the boy, as under the weight of an enormous, mysterious pain!

Meanwhile, Mgr. Stumpf took an image from his breviary and offered it to the child, who repelled it with violence. Monsieur Tresch, however, held him tightly griped in his arms: Then Mgr. Stumpf placed the pictured image on the child's head. The boy violently shook his head until the image fell from it. This action seemed to tire the poor patient very much. He perspired and wiped his face with both his sleeves. His breathing became difficult.

While this was going on, little Joseph had jumped out of the window, and went to play with his little brothers and Sisters in front of the house.

The mother gives interesting details about the boys. They were always good and were very fond of school. Four years ago, coming from their class, their behaviour changed mysteriously. Thiebaut had convulsions during the night, especially at 10 o'clock and at midnight. His voice was not the same and he lost consciousness. His tone in speech had become a hoarse bass and it remained so during all the four subsequent years.

The Commission of Enquiry left the house about noon. Their mind was made up. They had witnessed the abnormal condition, under which the boys were labouring, and gained the conviction that it was a case of diabolic possession. Monsieur Tresch went to see the children at 10 o'clock that same evening. "Do you know," he asked, "the rev. gentlemen who called on you today,"

"You say gentlemen ! I am myself a greater gentleman!"

"Where do they come from ?" asked Monsieur Tresch.

"One," answered the boy, "from Mulhouse, not far from here!"

"Which one?" asked Monsieur Tresch.

"The one," answered the boy, "who often went out, and who had not a very strong opinion about my case. But the two others have a very strong and firm wrist !"

"What about the one who presented you with a picture?" queried Monsieur Tresch. "Where does he come from?"

"From Strasbourg," replied the boy. "He is doing me most harm. The *cleric with the great cap* [meaning the mitred bishop] has sent him!"

"And the third gentleman!" continued Monsieur Tresch.

"He comes from Enisheim," replied the child. The poor boy was deaf, but the parents did not know it. He told me, "I am going to find ways and means to put you off the track, and to render you incredulous alike with Mgr. Stumpf."

Letter written by Monsieur Tresch to Mgr. Stumpf, April 15, 1869.

THE END.

Made in the USA
Monee, IL
11 January 2022